M000021293

MASTERING YOU FROM THE INSIDE OUT

SURVIVE AND THRIVE,
PERSONALLY AND PROFESSIONALLY

4/15/20

Elly —

Thank you for being such a great friend for Barbra. Hope you enjoy the book!

Skip C

SKIP CUMMINS

Copyright © 2019 Skip Cummins

All rights reserved.

No part of this book may be reproduced, stored in a retrieval system, or transmitted by any means, electronic, mechanical, photocopying, recording, or otherwise, without written permission from the author.

Disclaimer:
This book and its contents represent the opinion of the author and is in no way intended to be interpreted as a guarantee. The author highly recommends that you educate yourself before investing.

Published by Mastering You LLC

Cover and Interior Book Design by GKS Creative
www.gkscreative.com

Edited by Jared Kuritz, Shelley Chung, and Kelly Davis

First printed in the United States of America

ISBN: 978-1-948792-10-3 (Ingram paperback)
ISBN: 978-1-948792-12-7 (KDP paperback)
ISBN: 978-1-948792-13-4 (eBook)

Library of Congress Registration Number TXu 2-158-226

Dedication

To Grandma Bowie and all those like her, past, present and future

TABLE OF CONTENTS

CHAPTER 1
MY STORY

IF I ONLY knew then what I know now . . . or had a confidante who did. In the spring of 1987, at the age of thirty-three, I saw, smelled, tasted, and felt death for the first time. Not just anyone's death. My mother's death. Not a peaceful passing, but a murder. A suicide in which my mother murdered herself. Probably by taking an overdose of phenobarbital combined with cheap vodka. She tragically took her own life and died alone, lying naked on a bare mattress in a small, dark apartment in my hometown of Grove City, Pennsylvania, with garbage, fast-food wrappers, and a sea of cheap vodka bottles two feet deep on the floor. Nobody deserves to die such a terrifying and lonely death. Especially not a mother. Not yours, not mine.

I will never forget what I experienced that day. My mother's total despair, anguish, and hopelessness penetrated every fiber of my being and pierced the depths of my soul. I was overwhelmed by shame and guilt for not somehow stopping my mother. For not knowing. For not getting her the help she so desperately needed. I was paralyzed by the utter anguish my mother and others like her must have felt in the years, months, days, minutes, seconds, and in the last breath prior to their suicides.

I later learned that more than 35,000 Americans like my mother commit suicide every year. Yet suicide remains one of the most underreported causes of death. Why underreported? Shame and guilt, and suicide isn't covered by most life insurance policies. My mother's death certificate doesn't show suicide as her cause of death. It showed heart failure, which was the literal and figurative truth.

Based on the advice of the Mercer County coroner, an old high school friend of mine who called to inform me of my mother's death, I didn't notify my two older sisters until after I arrived at my mother's apartment and saw how much I needed to do to protect my sisters from knowing the horrible way in which my mother was living and how she had died. Once I called them, I had twenty-four hours to dispose of all the sights and smells that told the story—all the trash, the mattress covered in my mother's bodily fluids, the carpet, my mother's clothes that couldn't be dry cleaned, her upholstered furniture, drapes, etc. I don't recall much of those twenty-four hours other than it was nonstop cleaning, making runs to the dump, and sobbing. I also recall that regardless of how much Pine-Sol and Lysol I breathed in, I couldn't get the smell of my mother's horrible death out of my nostrils, let alone my being.

To say that my mother's life was a struggle is an understatement. She was an only child whose salesman father committed suicide by jumping off the roof of a hotel in Chicago when she was sixteen. She was disowned by her mother for marrying my father. She worked all of her adult life, first as a welder during World War II in the local factory. After the war, she became a nurse. She had an extreme love-hate relationship with my father that produced countless verbal, emotional, and physical battles; two daughters and one son (me); one stillborn daughter; and three marriages and three divorces—to and from each other.

To help her deal with her depression and emotional pain, my mother wrote herself illegal prescriptions and became addicted to phenobarbital, a very powerful barbiturate. In 1960, she was caught and arrested in front of me in our small house by one of my best friends' fathers, who was a justice of the peace. She was immediately taken to jail, then sentenced to six months of cold-turkey addiction "recovery" in the rather notorious Pennsylvania State Hospital for the Insane in Warren, Pennsylvania. "Interventions" in those days often involved straitjackets, electroshock, and other forms of "treatment." I was six years old and wasn't allowed to visit my mother when she was in the "hospital," but my oldest sister, who was sixteen at the time—ironically the very same age my mother was when her father committed suicide—recalls bursting into tears when, on one of her first visits, she saw my mother sitting outside on a bench in a straitjacket, totally comatose.

My mother's courage was incredible. After she came home to the small, very religious and highly judgmental small town of 5,000 people where we lived—and where she was a known criminal, drug addict, and resident of "Warren"—she started selling Avon door-to-door. She was incredibly successful. Every month, the products needed to fulfill her orders filled the entire first floor of our small house. She was soon promoted to district manager and moved to central Pennsylvania. She had a new Oldsmobile, her dream car, every two years. She joined a country club and was regularly swimming and playing golf, which she loved.

Unfortunately the pressure of her job and her loneliness made her easy prey for the lethal combination of a pathological liar and sociopath after her money, and her depression and addiction demons. She was fired from Avon and returned to Grove City—a broken woman. When she couldn't take the pain anymore, she chose the only quick and effective treatment she knew that ultimately brought us back together in Grove City for the last time. During her funeral in the spring of 1987, I vowed to do whatever I could to give those suffering from severe depression an alternative to the one chosen by my mother. For their sakes and the sakes of their loved ones.

Little did I know what my vow had in store for me. Eight years later, the opportunity to honor my vow appeared when I became the CEO of Cyberonics, Inc., a struggling start-up that was trying unsuccessfully to pioneer entirely new science regarding the vagus nerve and a revolutionary new implantable device called the vagus nerve stimulator. The company was approaching figurative bankruptcy in every way. The FDA had just turned down the company's first request for approval of the nerve stimulator to treat epilepsy, half the company's management and employees had resigned, the company had little remaining cash, and its public market value had dropped to under $25 million.

Consistent with my personal vow to my mother, the first thing I did at Cyberonics was create and align everything we did with a new company mission to improve the lives of people touched by treatment-resistant epilepsy and other disorders, e.g., depression that proved to be treatable with our device. After raising additional capital, hiring new management, and completing another epilepsy study, we finally had FDA approval for the device, not drug, for people with drug-resistant epilepsy. Clinical studies and commercial use showed remarkable sustained and improving long-term effectiveness and safety, so much so that the vagus nerve stimulator became the fastest-selling new active implantable device in history.

Not unlike most breakthrough treatments, we were curious whether our unique device might effectively treat other treatment-resistant illnesses. Doctors' reports of mood improvements in epilepsy patients and brain imaging studies strongly suggested that those with treatment-resistant depression, like my mother, could benefit! Encouraged by these observations, we embarked on a multiyear clinical study to prove the long-term safety and effectiveness of our device in patients with by far the worst depression ever studied, namely those treated for depression for an average of fifteen years unsuccessfully with an average of eighteen different treatments, including multiple drugs and ECT (electroconvulsive therapy, aka electroshock). In what many thought was a hopeless patient population with no chance of responding, the vagus nerve stimulator produced unprecedented sustained and improving safety and effectiveness over two years, including reductions in suicidal ideation and suicides!

The big difference, though, was that roughly four million Americans suffer from treatment-resistant depression, ten times the number that suffer from drug-resistant epilepsy, and the anti-depressant drug market is one of the largest and most profitable drug markets in the world. In other words, our attempt to change the status quo to give Americans like my mother an alternative to suicide would threaten some of the most powerful people, companies, and institutions in the United States, including Big Pharma, the FDA, senators, Wall Street, insurance companies, and Medicare.

Like something out of a Hollywood movie, our product, and especially me as its spokesperson and passionate champion, suddenly became "enemies of the state." Despite—or more likely because of—(1) having the support of numerous psychiatric thought leaders, experts in treatment-resistant depression, and patient advocacy groups; (2) having conducted unprecedented long-term studies of patients with by far the worst depressions ever studied; (3) having proved that drugs didn't work in patients with severe depression; and (4) having successfully overturned the FDA's initial not-approvable decision with the support of numerous senators and members of congress, vagus nerve stimulation and I became the subject of vicious attacks, intense investigations, false allegations, and sensational inaccurate reports, one after another. Certain FDA personnel, US senators, insurance companies, Wall Street, Medicare, the *New York Times*, etc., seemed to have decided it was time for me and vagus nerve stimulation for treatment-resistant depression to disappear. Although the facts and data were overwhelmingly on our side and some four million Americans desperately needed an FDA-approved alternative to suicide, we clearly didn't stand a chance versus the very powerful people who controlled the status quo Cyberonics and I threatened.

Despite Cyberonics' annual sales having grown to over $125 million, its public market value having exceeded $1.2 billion, and the Epilepsy Foundation having given me a lifetime achievement award, one year after the FDA approved the nerve stimulator's use to treat depression, my reputation, career, and net worth were destroyed by false allegations of options backdating by a third-tier Wall Street research analyst that triggered an SEC inquiry. Although I was found to have done nothing wrong, I was forced to resign from the company I built with the mission I created to improve the lives of people with treatment-resistant illnesses. Worse yet, shortly after my departure, the vagus nerve stimulator—the only FDA-approved treatment for treatment-resistant depression—was no longer available to people like my mother who desperately needed an alternative to suicide.

After ten years of unwavering passion for and commitment to Cyberonics and its mission, I was devastated by my forced resignation and how it was handled. I was not allowed to review the options report commissioned by Cyberonics in response to the SEC inquiry. The board of directors refused to meet with me and instead had the company's SEC lawyer ask for my resignation. My freedom of speech and right to publicly defend myself against the many false allegations that were made against me were taken away not only for the six months before and immediately after my resignation, but also for the ensuing five years until I received a closure letter from the SEC. Although I knew every employee, almost all the doctors that used our product, hundreds of patients, many of Cyberonics' investors, etc, I was prohibited from communicating with anyone associated with Cyberonics or its product, even to say goodbye.

Last but not least, under a figurative cover of darkness on a Sunday morning when the company was closed, I was allowed to collect my personal belongings from my office under the supervision and watchful eye of the company's vice president of human resources, whom I had previously hired and who had reported to me as CEO.

I needed a small U-Haul truck to transport the largest of my possessions, a large, brightly colored painting of a cowboy that looked like Teddy Roosevelt sitting on a horse holding an American flag, home. The painting has no background and no foreground and is called *The American Dream*. I bought it in the '90s from an artist who had lost his commercial graphics company and his wife to an untrustworthy partner. As I drove away from Cyberonics for the last time, it dawned on me that my American dream, just like the artist's, now had no background and no foreground. It was hard to see the road through my tears as my thoughts once again returned to my mother's apartment and the horrible sights, sounds, and smells of her despair, hopelessness, and suicide. Thank god I had a wife, daughter, and son whom I loved and who loved and needed me.

In the days and years since that fateful Sunday just before Thanksgiving in 2006, I have often reflected on the invaluable lessons I learned there, on my journey since, and my life prior. In other words, I rediscovered the background and foreground of my American dream, full of victories, defeats, accomplishments, failures, and mistakes. Lessons from being raised on $12.50 a month in child support by my figurative "Grandma" after my parents' third and final divorce from each other. From daring to dream big and becoming the first person from my hometown to attend an Ivy League school, Dartmouth College, where I was an All-Ivy linebacker and javelin thrower. From watching my mother struggle with lifelong prescription painkiller and depression demons. From working all sorts of jobs, including road construction, pizza cook, a commercial lender who first made then collected loans, venture capitalist, public company chairman and CEO, and certified tantra educator. From marriages of eighteen and twenty-one years. From inspiring and helping my children, now grown, realize their respective dreams of becoming a veterinarian and playing major college football. From having everything I worked for my entire life, most importantly my dream of helping people like my mother, taken away from me. From the validation and rewards that come from having an unwavering commitment to improve the lives of others. And from a journey of introspective and brutally honest awakening and empowerment that has enabled me to own, embrace, learn from, and be grateful for every one of my successes, failures, and mistakes.

I've often pondered, "If I only knew then what I know now." My conclusion, regardless of the "then" to which I'm referring, is that my life, my family's lives, and the lives of hundreds of thousands of people touched by treatment-resistant illnesses, including epilepsy and depression, would be considerably better if I knew then what I know now, or had a confidante who knew then what I know now.

So here we are. At the end of the beginning of my first book, which is in part inspired by my *American Dream* painting hanging on the wall in front of the desk where I sit writing. True to what continues to be my personal mission of improving the lives of others, I'm writing this book to share with you all that I know "now" regarding business, relationships, managing conflict, understanding who and what you are, effective communication, picking your battles, the importance of integrity, changing status quos, living your intentions and boundaries, creating and achieving financial goals, embracing and owning mistakes, and creating extraordinary happiness and abundance for you and your family so that in the future you say, "If I only knew then what I know now" a lot less frequently than I have.

CHAPTER 2

THE ORIGIN CHALLENGE

Know from whence you came to maximize your opportunities and success in the present and future.

IMAGINE AN ATHLETE who played the same sport and same position and had the same coaches for eighteen years. Wouldn't that athlete be totally programmed to do everything the same way every time without having to think about it? No thinking required. Just doing as they were programmed by eighteen years of coaching by the same coaches, by eighteen years of analyzing every second of their performance in training and in competition. Training meaning every aspect of how they were living their lives. When they slept, when they awoke. What they ate. How they mentally prepared. How and when they trained. Their relationships with teammates, the media, their coaches, fans, friends, their significant other. On and on. A human computer, programmed to consistently perform in a certain way.

Although my example is an extreme one, guess what? You and I and every other human being on the planet is in many ways the athlete I described above. We have all been programmed by our experiences during our first eighteen or so years of life, our primary "coaches" being our parents and our secondary coaches being teachers, friends, other family members, sports coaches, and our experiences. An awful lot was invested by a lot of people in our programming. We might as well maximize the return on that investment by not living in the past but understanding from whence we came and using that knowledge to create the best versions of ourselves and the brightest present and future possible.

Here is an origin challenge exercise that will illustrate my point:

1. Write down five to ten words or phrases that immediately come to mind to best describe your mother during your childhood. Don't think about whether they're positive or negative. Just write down what immediately comes to mind, such as loving, caring, compassionate, happy, supportive, understanding, patient, affectionate, dedicated, positive, polite, respectful, fair, strong, reasonable, trustworthy, honest, creative, inspiring, successful, hardworking, away from home a lot, emotionally unavailable, angry, unhappy, critical, mean, liar, self absorbed, negative, resentful, jealous, disciplinarian, strict, constantly yelling, selfish, and physically, emotionally, or sexually abusive, etc.

2. Do the same for your father.

3. Now write down three to five things that you wish your mother had done more or less of to be a better mother.

4. Do the same for your father.

5. Now write down five words or phrases that best describe your parents' relationship.

6. Now write down three to five of your positive personality traits that have been communicated to you by personality profiles you've taken or by bosses, friends, current and former significant others, your kids, etc.

7. Do the same for your personality traits that you or others think you need to change for the better.

8. Write down five words or phrases that best describe your current marriage or relationship and a prior marriage or relationship.

9. Compare your lists with the lists you made for your parents. What are the similarities and differences? Do you see how your lists for your parents may have programmed you to be the way you are and caused your relationships to be the way they are?

Now that you've done my quick origin challenge exercise, how much do you think your experiences or your nonexperiences before age 18 influence your actions, reactions, emotions, feelings, fears, triggers, strengths, and weaknesses as an adult? Think about opportunities you haven't fully taken advantage of and what caused you to miss those opportunities. Think about times when you found your behavior or something you said to be baffling; when you asked yourself, "What was I thinking?" or "What in the world motivated me to do or say that?"

My personal experience would suggest that seemingly inexplicable behaviors and choices that resulted in lost opportunities are explained by a combination of three things. First, your life experiences prior to age eighteen, which created patterns of behavior, thoughts, feelings, emotions, fears, reactions, and triggers. Second, your lack of understanding of this origin programming, and, third, your failure to do appropriate adult reprogramming.

After I left Cyberonics, I began studying and teaching tantra yoga, and living as an "untethered soul" as described in Michael Singer's outstanding book by the same name. I thought I had let go of my experiences as a child and that those experiences had little to do with me as an adult. I could not have been more wrong. ALL my of successes and failures and ALL the things I could have done better to create more abundance for the people and world around me before, during my time at, and after Cyberonics were predicted not only by my experiences through age eighteen, but also by my failure to understand from whence I came and overcome my origin challenge.

As I share with you some of my more provocative observations and experiences regarding from whence I came, think about your own. Keep in mind that strengths can quickly become weaknesses when your inner child's patterns become those of a more powerful, better educated, stronger adult, and, in some cases, the "Incredible Hulk." And remember that like history, which we are destined to repeat unless we know it, becoming an awakened and empowered adult master of our energies, actions, and words requires that we know and understand from whence we came and overcome each of our origin challenges.

It often takes a major adult trauma to motivate us to look deeply within ourselves and discover from whence we came. To discover who and what we really are and why. One of my many reasons for writing this book is to help you overcome the origin challenge and use your from whence you came programming to realize your full potential . . . without wasting opportunities and enduring the tragedy and trauma that gives you no real choice.

My major adult trauma was my humiliating forced resignation from Cyberonics that obliterated my identity, everything I believed in, and everything I had created and accomplished in my life. I felt completely worthless until my former wife introduced me to tantra and I decided it was time for me to rediscover my identity and truth without Cyberonics, from the inside out. There are many different forms of tantra. And many alternatives to tantra to discover who and what you are, what makes you happy, etc., from the inside out instead of what's given to you and taken away by the outside world. The tantra I studied, taught, and continue to practice helps us become awakened and empowered masters of our energies by first teaching us how to let go of negative energy blocks—"baggage" from the past—then helping us discover, summon, and use the extraordinary power within us. In other words, by first helping us understand, and when appropriate, let go of from whence we came and our origin programming. Or only use it when appropriate. Tantra is ancient Tao and Hindu forms of meditation, yoga, breathing and sounding techniques, and massage that, according to modern science, modulates certain areas of the brain and certain neurotransmitters. What modern science? Vagus nerve stimulation! No wonder I embraced tantra.

In order to truly understand from whence you came, you must be willing to be open and vulnerable regarding your past—brutally honest and nonjudgmental and trust that whatever you discover about your past will help you create a better you, present and future. Think about the times when you felt unloved, abandoned, betrayed, abused in some way, stupid, or incompetent.

Those times—unless you've forgiven those responsible, let go of them, and no longer allow them to control your life—are holding you back. As I used to tell my son when we were mountain biking and kart racing, "Look where you're going, not where you've been," and, "You won't finish, let alone win any races, driving in the rearview mirror."

So let's take a look at my origin challenge exercise and the impact that my failure to understand and adjust my origin programming and from whence I came had on many lives:

1. My mother was gone most of the time. Physically and emotionally unavailable. Consumed by her addiction demons. Good at selling Avon and good at golfing. Nice when she took me swimming. Always mad and yelling at my father. Hated hunting and fishing.

2. My father was a hard worker, funny, laughed a lot, a prankster, loved hunting and fishing, loved watching sports, especially me playing sports. Cooked great hamburgers. But emotionally unavailable. Crazy about my mother except her constant yelling and addictions.

3. My mother could have been a better mother first and foremost by not abandoning me, and by not convincing me that my needs didn't matter. She could have also loved and cared for me and been involved in every aspect of my life, including school, my grades, my sports, coming to all my games and track meets, my nutrition, helping me prepare for and choose a college, my social development. Like the mother of my children has done for our children.

4. My father could have been a better father by telling me all about his and his/my ancestors' lives and teaching me everything he learned from his life. He also could have

been involved with more than just my sports. He didn't seem to care about my grades or if, and which, college I went to. He didn't understand the significance of me being admitted to Dartmouth and getting a big financial aid package.

5. My parents' relationship was love-hate to the extreme. I witnessed mostly the hate part. Combative, contentious, constant fighting, my mother physically and verbally abusing my father. Complete antithesis to the idyllic relationships I saw on *Leave it to Beaver* and other TV shows. Three marriages to and divorces from each other says it all.

So now let's take a look at the impact this origin challenge and from whence I came and, more importantly, my lack of understanding about this impact had on my choices, which adversely affected arguably millions of lives.

Tantra taught me that self-mastery from the inside out required that I accept the origin challenge and completely understand from whence I came. As part of that process, I needed to understand and own all my major mistakes and failures that could have been prevented by knowing from whence I came and making appropriate adjustments to my origin programming when required. I discovered that the "whence" from which I came contained a lot of painful shame, guilt, abandonment, betrayal—including self-betrayal—and distrust, but also self-reliance, passion, courage, strength, determination, and resolve. Thrice married and divorced parents who fought all the time, a mother who chose phenobarbital over me before I turned six, being raised by a figurative "Grandma," and growing up in a small judgmental town that discouraged ambition taught me some very hard lessons that I carried into adulthood. I feared abandonment.

I felt like my needs didn't matter. I gave all of myself in the hope of being worthy of love, affection, and attention. My disease to please translated into an insatiable need for gratitude from those to whom I gave "gifts." All of this programming, which I didn't understand or control, did significant damage to me personally and professionally and definitely caused me to miss several opportunities that few people ever have.

Being abandoned and largely neglected by my parents taught me that I could rely on and trust only me, myself, and I. I had no mentors growing up and neither my parents nor my siblings were involved in my life from the get-go. I learned that everything was up to me and that I was responsible for my mistakes, failures, successes, and accomplishments. My goals were all mine. My dreams were all mine. I quickly developed a Terminator-like work ethic and a burning ambition to get out of Grove City and make something of myself. Everything was highly personal. My mission in life became "showing the bastards," meaning that anyone who told me that I couldn't do something became a "bastard" who needed to be proven wrong. Sports became my truth—the game films and my brutally honest inner scoreboard always accurately reflected how hard I worked and how well I performed. I didn't need to just win; I needed to dominate and absolutely crush my opponent. The bigger the challenge, the greater the risk and odds against me, the greater my commitment and determination. What did I have to lose?

Our fathers and mothers are major determinants of from whence we came and our patterns of behavior, feelings, and thoughts as adults. My father came from a long line of hard-working, poor, high-school educated, military veterans who didn't much care for the government, those in power, or "rich bastards." My father and Uncle Joe were best buddies. They both served in the Pacific in World War II, my father in the army, and my Uncle Joe in the Marines. I spent a lot of time with them as a kid, hunting, fishing, and listening to them emphatically agree on many things. They agreed that the entire world, including the United States, was controlled by a secret society called the World Leaders Club composed of the ten richest men in the world. They told me that World War II was fought for one reason—to make the Roosevelts and their fellow members of the World Leaders Club richer. Of course, neither of them trusted the government, politicians, or anyone with money because those people were working for the World Leaders Club and didn't give a damn about the working class who did all the work and fought all the wars. I used to joke about my dad's and Uncle Joe's theories until my demise at Cyberonics began, at which time their theories weren't so funny.

My reliance on me, myself, and I taught me that if I wanted to go places, which I did, I better work harder than everyone else to get there. And I better learn how to coach myself and own and learn from my mistakes. Of course, I learned a lot from my parents, Grandma, coaches, teachers, and friends, but I also embraced personal accountability and integrity at a very early age. If I lied or cheated, I was lying to and cheating myself and compromising my ability to get to where I wanted to go.

From whence I came was the fuel that enabled me to excel academically and athletically at Dartmouth, graduate at the top of my business school class, build a successful career in the venture capital business, and enjoy a wonderful personal life. But then came my mother's suicide and the much bigger Cyberonics' stage with significantly more complicated challenges, much more powerful and richer "opponents," and much greater risks and returns.

It was as if me, myself, and I and from whence I came went from high school football directly to the NFL professionally and personally. What I know now that I didn't know then is that my from whence I came strengths before Cyberonics ultimately became career-destroying weaknesses because I didn't understand the limitations of from whence I came and didn't change my game plan to win a much more challenging game against much stronger competition. The saying, "When under stress, people retreat deeper into that which they know" is exactly what I did at Cyberonics, much to my and people with treatment resistant illnesses' detriment.

My from whence I came strengths also enabled Cyberonics under my leadership to overcome one seemingly insurmountable challenge after another and to pioneer and commercialize new medical science and a revolutionary new device-based therapy that improved hundreds of thousands of supposedly hopeless lives. However, my "show the bastards" attitude didn't ultimately work well with Wall Street, insurance companies, FDA staffers, the media, senior senators, or board members. It also resulted in me focusing on being right, and fighting every fight instead of picking my battles carefully and staying focused solely on Cyberonics' mission and goals. Unfortunately, I made everything personal. Definitely not a good idea because at Cyberonics, we were changing the status quos from which many powerful people, companies, and institutions reaped considerable personal, professional and financial profits.

To be the most effective leader possible and give Cyberonics the best chance of succeeding, I should have recognized that my childhood programming strength was actually a weakness and revised it accordingly. Instead of relying on me, myself, and I and being the tip of the spear in every fight, I should have delegated, especially the more contentious tasks, to various Cyberonics vice presidents, board members, and lawyers. Instead, my reliance on my origin programming put a bull's eye on my forehead and made me a mortal enemy of some very powerful people. I also should have kept Cyberonics and my battles, especially with our more powerful opponents, under the radar and out of the public eye and ear. Instead, I believed that we would convince, or, if necessary, intimidate and thereby "show the bastards" if we simply provided all our data and then exposed what we considered to be our opponents' disregard of various regulations and the needs of millions of Americans. You have to be kidding me.

Understanding from whence you came is also extremely important when it comes to your personal relationships as an adult, especially with your significant other and your children. While studying and teaching tantra, I realized that most of us underestimate the extent to which we carry around baggage from the past and the impact that baggage has on our everyday lives and decisions. Many women I coached in tantra hadn't received the love or approval they wanted and needed as young girls from their fathers or mothers. Some had been physically, emotionally, or sexually abused by parents, family members, lovers, and husbands. To get the love and approval they didn't receive earlier in life, many of these women became promiscuous and/or gave up their power and voices to express their wants and needs and say no. Some turned to alcohol or drugs to ease their pain. Instead of finding the love including self-love they were looking for, they accumulated incredible amounts of shame and guilt and, in some cases, self-loathing, all of which was preventing them from reaching their full potential. While helping these women understand and let go of from whence they came, reclaim their power and voices, and discover their inner beauty, magnificence, and abundance, I was awestruck by our power and responsibility as parents. Although my young adult children were raised in a loving and supportive home, and were realizing their dreams of becoming a veterinarian and playing major college football on a full scholarship, based on my new appreciation of the importance of "from whence you came," I became a better parent. I began having more conversations with them instead of grilling them as if I were judging them. Whenever I offer advice, I try to offer that advice in support of what they're doing instead of advice motivated by them doing something wrong. I'm trying to share with them as I would share with a friend. And I'm trying to always tell them I love them and am proud of them.

Understanding from whence you came and from whence your significant other, partner, or spouse came is also very important so the two of you can effectively communicate as partners and defuse potential arguments. Understanding your respective origin challenges will also enable you to work together to let go of what doesn't serve you from your pasts and discover and share all the incredible beauty, power, pleasure, and bliss within you. The sooner the two of you understand from whence each of you came, the better your communication, the more compassion you'll have for each other, the more you'll love each other, and the more you can honor, nurture, and, when appropriate, forgive each other. My last marriage of twenty-one years ended in large part by us not understanding from whence each of us came, not controlling our accompanying fears and triggers, and not compassionately modifying our behaviors until it was too late. I didn't understand and fully appreciate from whence my former spouse came. As a result, I said, didn't say, did, and didn't do many things that triggered and hurt her, for which I am now sorry. Similarly, because I didn't understand my fear of abandonment, the feeling that my needs didn't matter, my disease to please, and insatiable need for gratitude, I hurt myself, my wife, and family by doing and saying things I never would have said or done if I knew then about from whence I came that I know now.

So what do you think caused me to make uninformed, poor choices and decisions that adversely affected not only me, myself and I, but also my family and the lives of millions of others? From whence I came and my origin programming, or my failure to understand from whence I came and overcome my origin challenge? My realization that it was my failure had almost as profound an impact on me as my mother's suicide and, as a result, produced a similar commitment: That being to own and learn from my failures, use what I know now to make better decisions going forward, and openly and honestly share what I know now to enable you to overcome your origin challenge and realize your full potential. Starting today. With full knowledge of the lessons from my life instead of waiting to have your life teach you those same lessons. And before you squander similar opportunities to create multigenerational wealth and happiness like I did. Too bad this book and I weren't available to help me master me from the inside out twenty-five years ago—like it is available to you today.

CHAPTER 3
YOUR HAPPINESS FORMULA

The sooner you master YOUR happiness formula, the sooner you will truly know what brings you happiness and why, and the more happiness you will create.

WHAT MAKES YOU happy? Having what you want? Having what you need? Having some of both? Who defines what you want and need and what makes you happy? Does what you need, want, and the things that make you happy come from without or from within? Think about everyone and everything that is trying to tell you what you want and need to make you happy. Your significant other, your kids, friends, neighbors, celebrities, professional athletes, work colleagues, doctors, salespeople, TV, radio, Facebook, Twitter, Instagram, the internet, email, smartphones, computers, billboards, authors (of course), politicians, motivational speakers, your boss. On and on. Nearly every second of every day, something or someone is trying to convince us of the things that we need and want. And that if we have those things, we will be happy. ALL from the outside in!

Real happiness can only be created from the inside out. It should be a reflection of the needs and wants that are important to YOU. Consider the following questions:

- Do you know WHAT makes you truly happy?
- Do you know WHY those things make you happy?
- Do you know HOW to apply these answers to create a formula that maximizes your happiness opportunities, takes full advantage of those opportunities, and creates extraordinary happiness for you and your family?

If your answer to those three questions is "yes" and your formula is working, great. But if you're not sure about some or all of these answers, want to see if you can improve a bit, or just want to try a proven formula, then keep reading.

Think of it this way: for many if not all of us, happiness is a choice. And every day we choose to not maximize our happiness is a missed opportunity. There are no tricks or gimmicks. It is simply a matter of you being honest with yourself, performing some introspection, and then making some conscious choices. Let's consider the happiness formula questions one at a time.

Question #1: What makes you happy?

I mean *really* happy. Take out a piece of paper or your phone and make a list of five things that immediately come to mind that make you happy. Be as specific as possible—personal, professional— like spending quality time with your kids, being intimate with your significant other, making money, hobbies, being successful at work, living in a nice house, being in good shape, driving an expensive car, financial security.

One of the many things I wish I knew then that I know now is that opportunities to create short- and long-term happiness come and go. Kids grow up. Marriages end in divorce. Jobs and careers end. Some are destroyed. Savings disappear. Income drops. Family tragedies like suicides, addictions, and major health problems occur. Etc.

Before my Cyberonics' demise destroyed my reputation, career, net worth, and most of my opportunities to create happiness, I thought I was happy. Very happy. Super happy. Personally and professionally. In every way I could imagine. Unfortunately, one of the most important things I didn't have was a fully informed happiness formula to create more happiness for myself and those around me each and every day. Sustainable happiness. I generally knew what made me happy, but I didn't know exactly why those things made me happy and what I needed to do to take full advantage of all the opportunities for more happiness—including lifelong and multigenerational happiness—that were within my grasp each and every day. I was too busy "listening" unconsciously to everyone and everything on the outside telling me what made me happy and what I needed to do to create that happiness—much of which made *them* happy by giving *them* more power and making *them* more money.

I didn't develop and begin to implement my happiness formula until I had no choice, namely once I began my journey to rediscover my identity four years after my humiliating forced resignation from Cyberonics. I was shocked by what I discovered. Because I had no happiness formula at Cyberonics, I had squandered more opportunities to create lifelong happiness for my family and me than I ever imagined. But, I also discovered that it's never too late to create happiness. I not only identified what made the Cyberonics and post-Cyberonics me really happy, but I also discovered my formula to create extraordinary happiness in almost any situation going forward. The self-inquiry process I went through was very similar to the questions I asked you at the beginning of this chapter.

My answer to the "what" question required me to consider what made me happy while I was at Cyberonics and what makes me happy now, given my past-versus-current opportunities for happiness. We all need to reconsider the whats, whys, and our formulas for happiness as we inevitably experience changes in our lives, including growing older, changing jobs, new relationships, etc. Needless to say, having my career, reputation, and net worth destroyed and becoming a retired, single, empty nester constituted some major life changes that required adjustments to my answers to the what, why, and how questions.

What made me happy before included (1) being a fearless warrior who overcame one seemingly insurmountable challenge after another and pioneered and commercialized new medical science and a device that improved hundreds of thousands of supposedly hopeless lives, (2) taking care of my family and being the best, most loving husband and father possible, (3) providing my family with the best of everything money could buy, including houses, cars, vacations, education, clothes, schools, private coaches, etc., (4) spending quality time parenting, teaching, and coaching my kids to help them make their dreams a reality, (5) looking good, feeling good, and being healthy, and (6) expensive hobbies like helicopter skiing and auto racing.

Now what makes me happy is similar but adjusted, given my new "life" and new, somewhat scaled-back opportunities to create happiness. First and foremost, what now makes me happy is financial security and living within my means. My "what makes me happy" list also includes (1) spending quality time with and being a great father to my grown kids, (2) taking care of, loving and being loved by my family including my former wife and the mother of my children, my significant other, friends, etc., (3) overcoming seemingly insurmountable personal and professional challenges, like writing this book and launching my new brand and business as a personal- and professional-development speaker, teacher, confidante, and coach, (4) improving peoples' lives, (5) maintaining good physical, mental, and emotional health, (6) being trusted and respected personally and professionally, and (7) vacations and entertainment that I can afford.

The second question to the happiness formula can be a little more challenging:

Question #2: WHY do those things make you happy?

Now that you have your short list of what makes you happy, write down at least three common reasons why those things make you happy. (Hint: consider the feelings these activities engender in you, such as validation, empowerment, and the feeling that you are a good person.)

Once I completed my lists of what made/makes me happy, I then debated what in the world all those activities had in common. Finally it came to me: Regardless of the activity, I felt as though time had stopped, meaning I was experiencing bliss. I also felt like I had earned— and deserved—whatever happiness I was experiencing in part because I was consciously with a positive purpose doing what I was doing. Last, I felt that my happiness wasn't taking anything from someone else or was coming at someone else's expense. In other words, I was happy doing whatever I was consciously doing that I knew would make me happy, stopped time for me, I felt I deserved and had earned, and didn't hurt anyone else. Bingo.

Can you recall the first time you experienced time-stopping bliss or thought someone else was doing something to stop time? What were you or that person doing? The first time I believed that someone had stopped time was when I first went to an Indy 500 practice session. As we neared the underpass to drive under the track and park in the infield, for the first time I heard the screaming engine of an Indy car approach and then fade quickly in the distance. I felt the sound and speed and knew that the driver of the 200 mph bullet had stopped time. With total clarity and certainty. And I knew the euphoria the driver must have felt. For me there is no greater happiness than totally losing track of time.

Once you have answered the WHAT and WHY, it's time for the action question.

Question #3: How are you creating the feelings that produce the happiness you feel when doing the things that make you happy?

Once I knew the answers to the "what" and "why" happiness formula questions, I asked myself, "What am I doing or could be doing better to produce more of those feelings that create my happiness?" Being a big believer in managing or coaching "inputs" to drive desired results, or outputs, I wanted and needed to know what were the common inputs that I provided to each of those situations to produce my specific feelings of happiness. In other words, consistent with "from whence I came" and doing the origin challenge, I was convinced that my happiness was the result of something that me, myself, and I did, not something that I was given.

After a few months of meditation and contemplation, including during sessions for my first tattoo which tells the story of my demise at Cyberonics and is shown on the cover of this book, my common inputs to produce my happiness appeared. In every situation in which I experienced happiness I had acquired a specific skill, worked hard to create the specific happiness opportunity, and was fully present with clear and focused integrity, intentions, and boundaries. I wasn't thinking about the past or the future. I wasn't trying to fool myself or anyone else. My intentions were pure, namely to do whatever I was doing well, without distraction and without hurting anyone else. Lastly I had clear boundaries that my inputs were more important than the outcomes of whatever I was doing and my inputs therefore couldn't be compromised.

What I discovered was that my inputs produced my happiness, not the specific activities I was doing or the results I was achieving. Consistent with Theodore Roosevelt's famous quote about daring greatly so that your place will never be among those cold and timid souls that know neither victory nor defeat, and quotes from Gandhi regarding the freedom and happiness that arise from pure motives and correct means and the renouncement of one's attachment to outcomes and results.

By far the most important happiness-creating input for me was being fully present in the moment, fully conscious of what I needed to do and not do to create happiness. Locked into and onto the present with total focus. In essence, living my happiness formula. Then moving on to the next "present" with total focus in a step-by-step acquisition of happiness.

Moving to California as a retired, single empty nester for the first time in my life significantly challenged my happiness formula in a couple of ways, primarily in terms of financial security and secondarily in terms of dating and relationships. Unfortunately while at Cyberonics, financial security and the accumulation of wealth and income-producing assets weren't on my "what makes me happy" list. It wasn't a concern because given the staggering salary and bonuses I was being paid, plus proceeds from stock sales, I could afford what I thought made me and my family happy, which was the best of everything defined by price, including houses, cars, hotels, vacations, hobbies, clothes. If I knew then what I know now regarding my happiness formula and the importance of sustainable financial security, my net worth would be more than twenty times what it is today and my family and I would be considerably happier.

The same is true if I knew before I moved to Southern California what I know now regarding my happiness formula. Almost everything in California costs at least twice what it costs in Texas, especially housing. To make matters far worse, not only does California have the highest income tax of any state, but also unlike the federal government and almost every other state in the country, California taxes municipal bond interest. As a result I paid 15% California income tax on what the federal government and most other states define as income! Inspired by my outrageously expensive California mistake, the writing of this book and my new-found happiness formula, I recently bought and moved to a house in a beautiful gated golf course community on the west side of Las Vegas. My total cost of living is now 75% below what it was in California. Not only does Nevada have no income tax and very low property taxes, but my monthly mortgage, homeowners insurance, and homeowners association payments are just slightly above my monthly Social Security benefits. Viva Las Vegas indeed! It's never too late to learn from your mistakes and failures, and create and implement your happiness formula.

In addition to convincing me that I had to leave to implement my new happiness formula, California taught me other valuable lessons regarding living within my means to achieve long-term financial security. Now I buy only what I need and I buy based on value, not price. Same for travel and vacations. Same for restaurants and entertainment. Getting a great deal now makes me happy. As does putting something back on the shelf that I've decided I don't really need. Costco, Southwest Airlines, Nordstrom Rack, Airbnb, and consignment stores have taught this old dog many new tricks that create financial security happiness for me.

I met many others in California who were taught the same lesson regarding the importance of understanding one's happiness formula and "running the numbers" before moving to California. Before you accept a promotion, agree to a transfer, take a new job that requires you to move to another state, especially expensive states like California or New York, make sure you know what makes you happy and compare your compensation, the income tax, property taxes, cost of housing, cost of insurance, cost of healthcare, etc., so that you make a fully informed decision regarding whether the move will truly make you happy. So you don't say after your move, "If I only knew then what I know now." Like I did.

Dating and relationships also challenged my happiness formula. After being married for twenty-one years living in Texas, I suddenly found myself as a stranger in a strange land. For the first time in my adult life, I was a single empty nester living in Southern California, giving online dating a shot. If ever there was a test for my happiness formula, this was it.

The distance between me and my happiness increased on my first couple of dates when some of my dates' photos were ten years and twenty-five pounds out of date, or all they talked about was their ex-husbands and/or their health and financial problems. "Inspired" by these first couple of dates, I said to myself, "Okay, Mr. Awakened and Empowered Master of Your Energies and Happiness Formula, let's see what you can do with this new reality." I figured that since I committed to invest my time and money, I might as well try to get a return on investment by testing my happiness formula. So what did I do? I let go of the past, meaning whatever—including their photos—was in their profile and focused on the present, meaning something we had in common: kids, funny online dating experiences, favorite vacation spots, hobbies like yoga, mountain biking. Lo and behold, even though I knew that we'd probably never see each other again, time stopped for a couple of hours, we had fun, and experienced bliss.

Of course, dates that challenged my bliss-creating skills inspired me to do a bit more due diligence upfront, such as having a video phone call so we both could make fully informed decisions about the present.

Ultimately, step three is the most challenging in this process. Making the necessary adjustments in your life so you can do the things that make you happy more frequently, more consistently, and to their fullest is key to creating and maintaining your formula. Easier said than done, I know. Rest assured that making these adjustments to your happiness formula and strengthening other aspects of your personal and professional life is precisely what this book is about. From setting boundaries to developing and living your plan, and everything in between, the activities in this book are designed to empower you.

One final important thing to keep in mind on this subject is that nearly all happiness formulas are different and they change over time. And there will be external influences that force us to adjust. And as we grow and change, so too do our priorities. This doesn't mean your old formula was wrong, it just means it needs to be recalibrated. Occasionally you will need to reassess what brings you happiness, why it brings you happiness, what you are doing to experience those feelings that bring you happiness, and adjust your approach to life accordingly. In fact, this is an incredibly good activity to do with your significant other from time to time. You two do not need have the same formula, but your formulas do need to complement each other and allow for the other to flourish.

Now that I've given you my story and happiness formula as an example, it's time for you to go back and answer the happiness formula questions and begin developing YOUR unique happiness formula. Do it with your significant other, kids and/or friends. You'll be amazed at what you learn about yourself and how much it will accelerate the mastering of you from the inside out. Once you know your formula, you will be able to create more short- and long-term personal and professional goals, evaluate your relationships, have a stronger foundation for managing the curveballs that life throws your way, and enthusiastically embrace each day as an opportunity for more happiness.

CHAPTER 4

THE INTEGRITY PRINCIPLE

"Integrity is doing the right thing when no one is watching" means that your integrity is up to you because you define the "right thing" and you are always watching.

SO WHAT'S YOUR definition of integrity? Do you follow the Golden Rule from the Bible and a maxim that can be found in almost every religion and culture, which is, "Do unto others as you would have them do unto you"?

Do you follow Polonius's advice from Shakespeare's *Hamlet* that goes, "This above all: to thine own self be true/And it must follow. . . /Thou canst not then be false to any man"?

Do you follow Machiavelli's philosophy (and the CIA's mantra when I was hired in 1976) that "the ends justify the means," meaning that so long as you have a worthy goal or "end," you can do whatever you need to do, use whatever "means" to accomplish that goal? According to *Psychology Today*, someone who is Machiavellian is "a person so focused on their own interests they will manipulate, deceive, and exploit others to achieve their goals." Sounds about right based on my experience, including with the CIA.

Write down your definition of integrity. What maxims, advice, philosophies, sayings, or rules do you follow? Once you have a list of "ingredients" that define your version of integrity, assign a percentage to each of those ingredients based on its relative contribution to your integrity definition, such as 100% Golden Rule, 50% Golden Rule and 50% Machiavelli ends justify the means, or 90% to thine own self be true and 10% "gut" instinct.

Once you've written down your definition of integrity and identified its relative ingredients, ask yourself whether the definition and ingredients have changed over time and how often they change. If your definition and ingredients constantly change, aren't you using Machiavelli's ends justify the means to define your integrity?

Now write down five lessons you've been taught during your life about integrity. Taught to you by yourself and by others. Lessons regarding good integrity and not-so-good integrity.

After examining your integrity, what do you think? How is it? How was/is your father's integrity? Your mother's integrity? How about your significant others', your spouse's, your kids', your friends integrity? How about your employer's integrity with its employees, customers, or its products? How about the integrity of the people you work with or do business with? Do you prefer people with integrity or those without? Who comes to mind as having high integrity? What examples of that integrity come to mind? Who comes to mind as having little integrity? What have they done—or not done—to support your opinion?

I have always been proud of my integrity, but my journey of self-mastery from the inside out and writing this book, especially this chapter on integrity, forced me take a long, hard look at not only my current and past definitions of integrity, but many of the lessons I've been taught about integrity. Here are a few of those lessons to guide you in mastering your integrity from the inside out.

I was taught from a very early age that integrity is very

important. People with integrity are trusted. People without are not. The dictionary defines integrity as "the quality of being honest and having strong moral principles." My experience says that integrity can also be defined as meaning what you say and do, and vice versa, and making sure that whomever you're dealing with has all the necessary information to make a fully informed decision. I've learned, often the hard way, that integrity is expressed by everything we think, say, and do. Everything. My definition of integrity has been and continues to be a combination of the Golden Rule and "to thine own self be true" from *Hamlet*. However, nobody, including me, is perfect and like most things discussed in this book, I wish I knew then what I know now about integrity.

I was raised by my Grandma Bowie. Not my real grandma but my mother's best friend's mother who became my "grandma" when, after my parents' third and final divorce, my oldest sister went with my mother, my middle sister went with my father, and I was the odd man/kid out. Grandma Bowie and the Southern Baptist church we attended were all fire and brimstone, especially when it came to the Golden Rule, telling the truth, and lying. Already afraid of burning in hell if I lied, Grandma Bowie appealed to my logic at a very early age. She told me that I shouldn't lie, because if I did, I would have to tell the same lie I told to one person to another five people, then the same lie I told to those five people to another twenty-five people, and so on until I had to tell the same lie to a million people. Her conclusion? Nobody's memory is good enough to tell the same lie to a million people, so don't lie. Just tell the truth. Who can argue with hell's fires and Grandma Bowie's logic?

While in Sunday school before church, when I was around seven years old, I was taught the importance of taking care of your integrity before you try to take care of someone else's. During a prayer, I opened my eyes and looked across the circle at my buddy Jimmy. His eyes were also open and when he saw me look at him, he started making really funny faces. It was all I could do to keep from laughing. After the prayer was over and we all dutifully said, "Amen," our seemingly 200-year-old teacher asked if anyone wanted to share anything from the prayer. I felt a need to report Jimmy's lack of prayer integrity, so I blurted out, "Jimmy had his eyes open," as I made a "gotcha" face at him. Our teacher turned and looked at and through me and quickly said, "How do you know?" Ouch! Nowhere to run. Nowhere to hide. Message and lesson received!

When I was a freshman in high school, Grandma Bowie reiterated the importance of integrity and the trust you earn when others believe in your integrity. The high school principal accused me of shooting several classroom windows with a BB gun. I told him the truth—that I didn't do it and didn't know who did. He nonetheless gave me detention. When I came home late and told Grandma Bowie why, she first ask me if I told the principal the truth and when I said, "Yes," she calmly said, "Then we'll have to pay the principal a visit tomorrow morning." The next morning, she and I were in the principal's office. The principal and I sat down. Grandma Bowie, all five feet two of her, stood leaning over the principal's desk, most definitely in his personal space. She asked the principal what happened, then asked me again if I told the principal the truth. When I once again replied, "Yes," she told the principal in no uncertain terms that she and I weren't going anywhere until he apologized to me for calling me a liar and giving me detention and apologized to her for wasting her time. We received our apologies and, as we were leaving, Grandma Bowie turned to the principal—who couldn't get us out of his office fast enough—and said in a voice loud enough for everyone in the office to hear, "Nobody accuses my grandson of being a liar! NOBODY!" Grandma Bowie could be very scary when she wanted to be, especially when she was teaching a valuable lesson on integrity.

It's fairly easy for someone to test our integrity, especially in today's world where there is no such thing as privacy and almost everything about each of us is somewhere on the internet. My fifteen years in venture capital taught me that the key to success is to find management teams with the right experience and skills to overcome seemingly insurmountable challenges. "Skills" including integrity. My first boss in the venture capital business had our administrative assistants verify every degree on the résumés of the management teams we were interested in. His theory? If someone lies about something insignificant like a degree from twenty years ago, they'll lie to you about anything and everything, especially when things get tough. Although 95% of the degrees were verified, I was still shocked that people would lie about something as easily verifiable as their résumés. Obviously, those people who lied about their degrees didn't get any money from us and no doubt had a hard time finding a job if any prospective employer checked their integrity, starting with their résumés.

There are lies by commission (telling an outright lie) and lies by omission (lying by withholding material information), neither of which we'd want "others to do unto us," and neither of which are being true to "thine own self." If you're in the business of selling things, which we all are given that we're always selling something—ourselves, our ideas, our company, products—don't you want as many satisfied customers as possible? How about "customers" who want to "buy" more from you and are great references?

At Cyberonics, our mission was to improve the lives of people touched by medically refractory epilepsy, treatment-resistant depression, and other disorders that might have proven to be treatable with our patented therapy, VNS. Patients and their families came first. Quarterly sales, profits, and our stock price came second, often to Wall Street's dismay. My intention as CEO was that Cyberonics' every employee's, and my own ethics and integrity would flow from our mission. Doing the "right thing" by doing unto others as we would have them do unto us was defined by our mission. If it was good for our mission, meaning the "right thing" for patients and their families, we did it. If it wasn't good for our mission, we didn't. Simple as that.

Our logic was simple nonzero-sum-game logic. In a zero-sum game, whatever one loses, the other wins. In a nonzero-sum game, if one party wins, all parties win; if one party loses, all parties lose. Our nonzero-sum-game logic was as follows:

- The more we accomplished our mission (the more patients' lives we improved), the more our sales and profits would grow and our stock price increase.
- The more our sales and profits grew and our stock price increased, the more of all Cyberonics' stakeholders, including employees and shareholders, personal, professional, and financial dreams would be realized.
- Our mission defined our primary "customer" as people whose lives were impacted by medically refractory epilepsy or treatment-resistant depression. The more satisfied customers we had, the more of our mission we accomplished.
- Our experience and all available data confirmed that the best and quickest way to create more satisfied customers, therefore accomplishing our mission, therefore increasing sales, profits, and the stock price, therefore realizing more of stakeholders' personal, professional, and financial dreams, was to enable patients and their treating physicians to make fully

informed decisions.

Creating fully informed customers was being true to ourselves and our mission. As a result, we created the first-ever long-term patient outcome registry in epilepsy. Our first-of-its-kind registry collected long-term seizure data, quality-of-life information, and information on side effects from doctors and their patient volunteers treated with our device following FDA approval. The purpose of the registry was to fully inform doctors and patients with the most up to date real-world experience, not just controlled pre-approval studies that were designed to obtain the most positive results possible. In other words, the registry would facilitate better-informed treatment decisions, not necessarily increase sales.

When I mentioned this idea to several doctors, they at first thought I was crazy. They explained to me that the reason drug companies didn't have similar registries was that treatment-resistant patients do not normally respond long term, so a registry would only sell *fewer* products, not *more*. Several of them went on to ask me, "Isn't your job as the CEO of Cyberonics to sell as much product as possible and maximize your profits and stock price?" My answer, which seemed to amaze them, was, "No, my job is to accomplish Cyberonics' mission of improving the lives of people touched by treatment-resistant epilepsy and other diseases, which means having our device used only on patients who are likely to benefit." Whether it amazed them or not, my words and Cyberonics' registry highlighted not only Cyberonics' commitment to our mission that put patients before profits, but also my integrity as CEO and the unique integrity of Cyberonics and its product. Our epilepsy registry, by the way, was an extraordinary success. By driving fully informed treatment decisions by doctors, nurses, patients and their families, it created one satisfied customer after another. Unlike drug continuation rates that were below 25% after 6 months of treatment, more than 85% of patients whose device reached end of service after three to five years elected to have a replacement device implanted! Which maximized our long-term revenues and profits! Which helped all stakeholders' personal, professional, and financial dreams be realized! Consistent with our mission, when the patients won, we won. Together.

Being unafraid to tell a customer or potential customer what the product you're trying to sell them is and equally importantly isn't is a way to showcase your and your product's integrity. Regardless of the "product," which among other things is always *you*. I recall that during a visit to a neurologist's office in North Carolina, the neurologist introduced me to one of his patients who wanted to meet the CEO of Cyberonics. The patient was a woman in her mid-sixties whose seizures prevented her from getting her driver's license but not from driving illegally. She had several seizures while driving without a license that resulted in a series of accidents that fortunately didn't result in any serious injuries. She was quite the character (she reminded me of Grandma Bowie) and when the neurologist finished telling me her story she said, "I'm so glad to meet you because I've heard that your VNS device will make me seizure-free and help me get my driver's license back."

Without hesitation I replied that VNS might help reduce the frequency and severity of her seizures and improve her quality of life, but there was less than a 10% chance that she would be seizure-free. I then showed her, the neurologist, and the nurse our registry data. After looking at the data, she said something to the effect of, "What kind of salesman are you?," to which I replied, "An honest one whose job is to help you improve the quality of your life, not sell more product." As we were leaving, the neurologist told me how incredibly impressed he was with my honesty and I immediately thought of Grandma Bowie. When I next saw the sales rep who had been with me that day, I asked him about the patient we'd met. He told me that based on our visit, the woman decided to go forward with VNS and while not legally driving, had experienced a significant decrease in her seizures and improvement in her quality of life.

One of the many benefits of writing this book is that, with each chapter, I've became a keener observer and student of my past and current selves and the previous and current worlds around me. Following my move to California from Texas, I discovered two totally different commitments to each state's process for creating fully informed buyers of residential real estate. In Texas, potential home buyers are given all the information necessary for them to make fully informed offers, *before* they make the offer. When I sold my last house in Texas, all interested potential buyers were given a spiral binder that included the MLS listing, a list of special features and recent upgrades, including the costs of each, the most recent survey, and the seller's disclosure. In California, buyers aren't given that information even if you request it until *after* there's a signed contract, by law. So let me get this straight: the state of California wants buyers and sellers to negotiate a purchase agreement *before* the buyers know everything they need to know to make a fully informed decision as to whether they want the house. Why would I as the seller want to waste my time with anything other than a fully informed buyer who *knows* that they want the house? Makes no sense to me.

My experience as a construction laborer, venture capitalist, public company CEO, certified tantra yoga teacher, friend, teammate, husband in two marriages totaling thirty-nine years, father, etc., has taught me that integrity is the foundation upon which every relationship is built. Most importantly, your relationship with yourself ("thine own self").

I learned a lot about integrity during my interviews with the CIA just after graduating from Dartmouth. My week-or-so-long interview process included many interviews, a lie detector test, multi-hour good guy/bad guy interrogation, psychological testing, etc. One of the things I learned is that the CIA generally operates under the Machiavellian credo "the ends justify the means," meaning that the CIA is justified in doing whatever it needs to do (the means) to preserve the national security of the United States (the end).

Included among the CIA's ends-justify-the-means operatives are "case officers" working out of our embassies around the world using a technique called "conscience expansion" to "recruit and manage foreign nationals to spy for the United States of America." Conscience expansion is a proven technique to, over time, get someone to incrementally redefine their integrity and ultimately commit treason. The easiest way to describe "conscience expansion" is that the case officer convinces the foreign national to do a little thing wrong for which they're compensated in some way, then the case officer expands the foreign national's conscience by convincing them to do ever more significant things wrong with ever more compensation of some kind until they are perfectly willing to provide the CIA with information that compromises their country's national security and potentially the well-being of their fellow citizens. If conscience expansion can cause people to commit treason, imagine what lesser wrongs it can convince us are justified, especially those of us whose integrity is defined by "the ends justify the means."

Many of us seem to be CIA case officers when it comes to expanding our own consciences to redefine our integrity, especially when it comes to committed monogamous relationships. One of the biggest mistakes I made and have observed others make is that they don't sit down with their relationship partners and define specifically what "committed" means, what constitutes "monogamy," and what constitutes "cheating."

Most no doubt agree that having sex with someone other than your committed, monogamous partner shows a lack of integrity, is not monogamy, and is cheating. CIA conscience expansion theory, and my own experience, confirms that cheating on your partner starts well before you have sex with someone else. Does it start with likes, comments, or messages on Facebook or Instagram? Does it start with a chance meeting and conversation in the grocery store with an old friend, a previous lover, a work colleague, a stranger? Does it start with having a drink, lunch, or dinner with the opposite sex? Does it start with you flirting with someone or accepting someone flirting with you? Does it start with you texting or talking to someone from your past just to catch up? Does it start when you and a previous lover hug on the street when you see each other for the first time in years?

Knowing what I know now, my "to thine own self be true" answer to those questions is that it depends first and foremost on the very specific definitions that my significant other and I have agreed on for monogamy, cheating, and integrity, which will include what behaviors and interactions are within the agreed-upon boundaries of our relationship. Boundaries that include limits on (1) to what extent we allow others into our respective consciousness, (2) our intentions, (3) the energies we share, and (4) our respective purposes and the purposes of the others we're interacting with for the interaction. For me it also depends on the Golden Rule and whether I would be happy if I witnessed my partner doing whatever I'm doing in similar circumstances and whether I believe she would be happy if she witnessed me doing what I was doing.

Having been married twice for a total of thirty-nine years and having witnessed many people being hurt by monogamous-relationship conscience expansion, I now finally have very strict definitions of monogamy, integrity, and cheating and what constitutes a committed, monogamous relationship. There are many types of "affairs," including sexual, emotional, intellectual, and spiritual, *all* of which take energy away from your partner in a committed, monogamous relationship and frequently destroy relationships and families, and hurt a lot of people who deserve a lot better.

One last comment about integrity, conscience expansion, and committed monogamous relationships is that many people justify their Macievellian integrity and affairs by demonizing their partners and/or rationalizing their ends justify the means approach to life and their cheating as something that everyone does, or even their partner did. What does that have to do with *your* integrity?

If I knew then what I know now regarding integrity, conscience expansion, and committed monogamous relationships, I would likely still be married to the mother of my children and still be the patriarch of a wonderful family.

So how do you feel about the idea that your integrity is defined by the Golden Rule and Shakespeare's "to thine own self be true?" Think about the last time your conscience bothered you about something you said or did. Did you consciously reflect on what was bothering you or did you immediately dismiss your cognitive dissonance? Did you ask yourself if you did unto the relevant others as you would have them do unto you? Were you true to "thine own self?" How do your answers to those questions make you feel now?

As I was writing this book, I started using the Golden Rule and the Shakespeare quote as an integrity check each time I had a difficult decision to make about the right thing to do. Those two simple questions: "Am I doing unto others as I would have them do unto me?" and "Am I being true to myself and telling myself the truth?" make decisions regarding integrity very easy. I also noticed that once I was being true to myself, it was easy to be true to others.

Having thought about your own integrity, what grades would you give the United States as a country, our institutions and leaders, and American society in terms of integrity? How about your kids, friends, coworkers, boss, and other family members? A, B, C, D, or F? How would today's grades compare to grades from five years ago? Ten years ago? Twenty years ago?

Which do you think more frequently defines integrity in the United States and in American society, the Golden Rule or Machiavelli's and the CIA's ends justify the means? It seems to me that our integrity is eroding when everyone acknowledges and accepts that US presidential candidates lie to get elected. News commentators use the politically correct term "fact checking" after the debates to count the lies by each candidate. Why not just say "lies" and stop the charade? I suppose because we are all trying to convince ourselves that it's okay for all candidates for the highest office in the land, the leader of the free world, and our commander-in-chief to repeatedly lie to the American people as a means to the end of being elected. What does the news media's, and our acceptance of this behavior say to the president-elect, to other politicians, to each other, to our children? It says that the "ends justify the means" is an acceptable arbiter of integrity. And that the president-elect, other politicians, the news media, you and I, and every other American including our children can do and say whatever we want so long as it's a means to an end that we deem worthwhile. How does that sound to you? Think about it the next time your teenager lies to you and justifies their lying by commission or omission as a means to an end of staying out of trouble and not upsetting you.

As I carefully examined my past and present integrity as part of my eight-year-long ongoing self-mastery journey from the inside out, I discovered that despite everything I lost, my integrity apparently remained largely intact. Several years after my career, reputation, and net worth were drop-kicked through the goalposts of life by the FDA, SEC, Senate Finance Committee, the Cyberonics board, Wall Street, etc., I asked a venture capitalist who was very well-connected in New York and DC what was the worst thing he'd heard about me. His response was that I was "principled to a fault." Coming from the epicenter of ends-justify-the-means integrity and Machiavellianism, I considered that to be one of the best compliments I ever received. To me, being principled to a fault is an oxymoronic impossibility.

So how about you? The outside world is trying to tell you many things including what your definition of integrity should be. Do you want to live in a Machiavellian world in which the ends always justify the means and most people "are so focused on their own interests they will manipulate, deceive, and exploit others to achieve their goals?" If not, as a major part of mastering you and your world from the inside out, find a definition of integrity that works for you and consistently live with integrity each and every day. As Grandma Bowie taught me, living with integrity is a lot easier than trying to remember which lies by commission or omission you told to whom and which of your many definitions of integrity you used when and with whom.

Don't you agree that with knowledge comes the responsibility to use that knowledge to master you from the inside out especially with regards to integrity?

CHAPTER 5

LIVE YOUR LIFE PLAN

Regarding business, someone once said, "What gets thoroughly planned, frequently measured, frequently reported, and appropriately rewarded, gets done." Isn't your life as important as business? Are you planning, measuring, reporting, and rewarding your life?

HAVE YOU HEARD the old saying, "Plan your work and work your plan?" How about, "Plan your life and live your plan?" That one you've probably never heard of because I just made it up. Why limit our planning to just work or business? Isn't life our highest priority in life? To achieve our full potential and live life to the fullest? If so, you and I need a plan for life that we frequently measure, frequently report, appropriately reward, and revise as necessary.

How many different types of plans have you created and/ or been a part of? Make a list. Business plans. Strategic plans. Travel plans. Party plans. Financial plans. Project plans. Treatment plans. Vacation plans. Wedding plans. Game plans. Study plans. All sorts of plans. How about a life plan? Do you have a plan for your life? To take advantage of the most opportunities, create the most happiness and abundance for yourself and those around you, avoid life-altering mistakes, and be prepared for life's challenges? Take Bill and Melinda Gates' challenge of giving away billions to worthy causes. According to Bill Gates, having a written philanthropy plan is essential because "the exercise of writing forces you to have logic and critical reasoning." If Bill Gates has a written plan to overcome the challenge of giving away billions, don't you think it would be a good idea for you to have a written life plan to overcome your life's challenges?

Here are a few questions, your answers to which will highlight whether you have the life plan I wish I had before my personal, professional, and financial opportunities of a lifetime were gone. Of course, as recommended by Bill Gates, writing down your answers is a good idea. Plan time frames should be at least one year.

- What are your relationship plans regarding marriage, cohabitation, kids, expenses, careers, housing, etc.? Including your relationship plan if you are creating a blended family from prior marriages.
- What is your career plan? Promotions? Job changes? Employer changes? Starting a company?
- What are your income, spending, and savings/investment plans?
- What is your housing plan?
- What is your car plan?
- What is your self-care plan? Exercise, vacations, meditation, hobbies, etc.?
- What are your parenting plans and your individual plans for each of your kids, regardless of age?
- What is your plan to keep your relationship/marriage growing and to honor, nurture, support, and love your significant other/spouse?
- What is your plan to take care of yourself physically, mentally, and emotionally?

- What is your plan to support your family, including parents, siblings, and in-laws?
- What is your plan to balance work and personal time to enhance your relationships with yourself and your family?

Doesn't every business you know do at least a one-year written business plan showing their goals and what they plan to do each quarter of that year (inputs) to achieve those goals? Every department in every company I've been associated with had their annual and quarterly goals and action plans of inputs to accomplish those goals. Quarterly meetings identified those departments and individuals who were and weren't achieving their goals and why. Departments and individuals that achieved and overachieved their goals were rewarded with bonuses, and in the case of the top-performing individuals in each department, an annual, one week, all-expenses paid vacation with their spouse/significant other called President's Club. Note that at Cyberonics, all employees were eligible for President's Club, not just salespeople, because our success as a company was equally dependent on all departments.

So are you planning your life and living your plan? Are you where you want to be, planned to be in life? Do you have the marriage or relationship you want to have, planned to have? Do you have the family you want to have, planned to have? Are you doing the work you want to do, planned to do? Are you making the money you want, planned to make? Do you have the savings you want, planned to have? Are you investing your savings to diversify your sources of income and maximize your income from sources other than your wages, salary, and bonuses the way you want, planned? Is your lifestyle what you want, planned? Are you as physically, mentally, and spiritually fit as you want, planned?

Are you and your family as happy as you want, planned?

I wish I had the same commitment to life planning as I had to business planning throughout my career. And I wish I had equally applied "what gets thoroughly planned, frequently measured, frequently reported, and appropriately rewarded" to my personal life as I did to Cyberonics. Had I done so, my family's net worth would be more than twenty times what it is today and my family and I would no doubt be sharing multigenerational wealth and happiness.

In the small town where I grew up, everyone was lower-middle class. I knew only one kid who had a swimming pool and maybe two who had more than one bathroom in their house. Most of the men in town, including my dad and uncles, worked at the only factory in town making union minimum wage building diesel locomotive engines. My dad never made more than $5,000 a year and he paid Grandma Bowie $12.50 each month in child support. I never set foot on an airplane until my senior year in high school. I think I went to maybe a total of five restaurants before I graduated from high school. Needless to say, I didn't know a lot about money and didn't know any "rich" people. My life goal when I graduated from high school was to be a quarterback in the NFL and if I couldn't do that, become a doctor. My plan for accomplishing my goals? Go to Dartmouth and work hard. Other than my dad constantly saying, "Money doesn't grow on trees," and mentioning "rich bastards," I didn't know anything about money and didn't know anyone who was "rich." As a result, money didn't figure in my plans.

Dartmouth opened my eyes to money even before I arrived in Hanover, New Hampshire. In 1971, when I applied, annual tuition, fees, room and board totaled approximately $25,000. I knew there was no way my dad could afford that. I also knew that Dartmouth didn't give athletic scholarships. Instead, Dartmouth offered financial aid (scholarships, loans, and a job) based on your parents' tax returns and what they could "afford" to pay. I was ecstatic when I received my admission and financial aid letters that informed me that my parents would only have to pay $1,500 per year. I ran upstairs and woke my dad, who was sleeping before he started the midnight shift later that night, to give him the great news. His response? "No rich bastards are going to tell me what I have to pay to send my son to college with a bunch of other rich bastards! Go to Slippery Rock!" As in Slippery Rock University, a state school in Pennsylvania only seven miles down the road that admitted everyone who applied my senior year in high school. After my stepmother calmed me down by informing me that yes I would go to Dartmouth, I deduced from my dad's commentary that I would probably meet "rich" kids at Dartmouth and get more acquainted with money.

When I arrived at Dartmouth, I quickly figured out that there were generally two kinds of kids there. "Preppies" from wealthy families who were paying full "retail" for Dartmouth and kids like me from poor families who were paying very little. For the first time in my life, I met a lot of people who came from money. I learned that real money afforded people a lifestyle the likes of which I never knew: houses with multiple bathrooms, expensive cars and clothes, private schools, incredible vacations. There seemed to be two ways to make real money: Inherit it or become a lawyer, doctor, or businessman like the fathers of the kids with money. If I didn't make it in the NFL, I was going to be a doctor, so no sweat.

Even though my dad was paying very little for me to go to Dartmouth, I needed spending money for pizza, clothes, contributions for beer at fraternity parties. During summers, I worked construction to make "big bucks," meaning $15.50 per hour, plus lots of overtime at time and a half or double time. During winter terms off, I worked near Breckenridge, Colorado, at the Pizza Hut to finance my education in skiing. While at Dartmouth, my post-graduation plans changed with my major and football position. After two weeks of not understanding a word the organic chemistry professor said, I quit organic chemistry and changed my major from pre-med to government with a specialty in international relations. My football position changed from quarterback to linebacker where I was a three-year starter.

Entering my senior year, I decided that I didn't want to play in the NFL and I didn't want to go to law school like most of the other government majors I knew. Instead, after an extensive interview process, I was hired by the CIA to what I thought was a position recruiting and managing foreign nationals to spy for the United States, but that I later discovered was special operations paramilitary work in Angola "defending" our oil interests. Most of the compensation was apparently in the form of excitement given that my GS pay grade paid only $14,000 a year. The CIA cancelled my job in September before I started, because Jimmy Carter was going to win the election in November and he didn't much care for the CIA.

Engaged to my Dartmouth girlfriend and living in Mahomet, Illinois, with my sister and brother-in-law working road construction at the time, I decided to get an MBA at the nearby University of Illinois since I had established residency in Illinois, an MBA would take only two years, and it wouldn't cost much. Two years later, after getting married and graduating with honors, I joined Continental Bank in Chicago as a commercial lending trainee making $23,000 a year. At age twenty-five, married with my first real job, neither my wife nor I had a plan. Predictably my consistent answer at that time to the series of life-planning questions I asked you at the beginning of this chapter was, "No clue."

As I look back on it, I find it rather astounding that I had an

MBA and was married to a Dartmouth grad who was in North-western business school getting her MBA and we had no agreement or plan for kids, careers, money, housing, cars, expenses, savings, or balancing work and personal time. I wish I knew then what I know now regarding life planning, which is that no plan equals one lost opportunity after the other in terms of relationships and abundance including financial abundance.

When I started work at Continental Bank with an MBA in finance, I didn't know much of anything about business including who made real money and how until a vice president at Continental's highly successful venture capital subsidiary gave a presentation to the commercial lending trainees. That presentation changed my life forever and redefined my personal and professional aspirations, intentions, and goals. I learned that entrepreneurs and venture capitalists founded, financed, created, and built some of the most successful companies in America, including Apple, Intel, Microsoft, and Federal Express. And that they made more money than I thought possible not from salaries and bonuses, but from equity, namely the stock they owned in their companies, which increased one hundred, two hundred, one thousand times in value. I *knew* that I had to become an entrepreneur or venture capitalist with equity to accomplish my personal and professional objectives that included having more money than anyone I knew in Grove City, Pennsylvania. Although I had a better idea of what I wanted to do for a living and the money I wanted to make, my wife and I still had no plan.

After two years in commercial lending at Continental Bank, I moved over to the bank's venture capital subsidiary in 1981. In 1984, after three years there, I joined Vista Ventures, a private venture capital fund, as one of four general partners. Not only was I now in venture capital, but I also had equity in the form of a percentage of the profits from what would become Vista's

$750 million of capital under management. Already known for my incredible work ethic, the equity opportunity and incentive at Vista inspired me to routinely work more than eighty hours a week and log over 300,000 miles a year traveling all over the United States and Japan. Every vacation was a working vacation. Vista was not my work; it was my life, a very profitable life. In 1986, my income exceeded one million dollars from salary, bonus, and equity distributions. I recall looking at my 1986 tax returns and thinking, "In only seven years since I started work at Continental Bank, my income increased to the point where I had to pay ten times my Continental Bank starting salary in taxes!"

At Vista I proved that not only was I good at investing Vista's money, but I was also good at helping the companies on whose boards I sat create, implement, and hold themselves accountable for the achievement of business plans to maximize revenues and profits and grow shareholder value.

Did I apply those same planning and investment skills to myself and my first marriage? "Aye, there's the rub," to quote *Hamlet*. Meaning, no I did not. My first wife and I had no personal financial and spending plan to diversify our sources of income or build sufficient wealth to sustain our lifestyle if our careers, for whatever reason, ended. To make matters worse, my first wife—who by then had her Northwestern MBA and a law degree from Columbia University—and I still had no agreement or plan for kids, careers, housing, cars, expenses, savings, income diversification, or balancing work and personal time. Because we had no life plan that we were frequently measuring, reporting, and rewarding, we made several major mistakes, the first and most significant of which was putting our careers ahead of our marriage, working long hours, abandoning what little intimacy we had, and living like roommates. The second being buying vacation homes in Vail and Maui that we used a couple of weeks each year instead of buying rental properties that we could use for the same vacations but would also produce significant income. The third being never discussing and agreeing on a plan for children, which increasingly became an issue for us; I wanted children, she did not. Having no plan meant significant opportunities lost and increasing conflict that ultimately destroyed our marriage.

I left Vista in 1995 as we were winding down our incredibly successful venture capital business and became the CEO of a struggling, publicly traded company called Cyberonics, one of Vista's portfolio companies. I also divorced, remarried, and started a family that ultimately included my then wife's daughter, Linda, whom I adopted, and who's now a veterinarian in Texas; and a son, Max, who is now on a full football scholarship at the University of Texas at Austin. Unlike my first wife, who was a lawyer, my second wife, Baiba, worked as hard as I was as CEO of Cyberonics as the CEO of our house and family, including two very active kids. We were great partners, both firmly committed to creating abundance on every level—emotional, intellectual, physical, financial—for our family and families. Although we agreed that we wanted to have at least one more child, we didn't create the kind of life plan I'm recommending that you create knowing what I know now.

Given the stakes and opportunity, my need for detailed professional career and personal life plans of which I rigorously implemented, followed, and achieved was considerably greater at Cyberonics than it was at Vista for three reasons. First, I now had a family to take care of, including two children who would eventually have families of their own. Second, as CEO of an early stage, publicly traded company, I was now an entrepreneur who had the opportunity to accumulate considerable wealth by pioneering and commercializing breakthrough medical science and technology that could improve hundreds of thousands of lives and create extraordinary shareholder value, including the value of my stock. Last, I knew from my experience in the venture capital business that the careers of early stage company CEOs rarely lasted longer than ten years, during which time the company failed or became so successful that it was acquired by a larger company, or the company became so large that it outgrew the entrepreneurial skills and experience of the CEO. In essence, I knew that my career as CEO of Cyberonics would, best case, be much like that of an NFL player. Meaning "not for long" and very profitable.

My lack of rigorous career and personal financial planning was a problem before Cyberonics. At Cyberonics, it was a disaster not only for me, but also for my entire family. Inexcusably, I squandered an opportunity of a lifetime to accumulate multi-generational wealth and income-producing assets to create an extraordinary quality of life for two to three generations to come.

Cyberonics was truly an opportunity of a lifetime for everyone involved. During my ten-year career there, we overcame one seemingly insurmountable challenge after another to accomplish our mission of improving the lives of hopeless people with drug-resistant epilepsy or treatment-resistant depression and create incredible value for all stakeholders, including shareholders. Over one hundred thousand patients' lives were improved. Cyberonics and I were awarded a Epilepsy Foundation Lifetime Achievement Award. Cyberonics' sales grew at an average of 50% a year over ten years and its stock price grew at an average of 35% a year over ten years. Cyberonics' total market value grew from $25 million when I joined to over $1 billion.

My salary, bonus, and the value of my Cyberonics' stock grew as rapidly Cyberonics' sales, stock price, and the number of lives we improved. My salary peaked at a mind-boggling $600,000 per year or $50,000 per month. My total salary and bonus peaked at over $1 million per year. Unfortunately, without a rigorous personal financial plan that recognized that my Cyberonics' career was the same as an NFL (not-for-long) player, I was spending 100% of what became my unsustainable salary and bonus just like many NFL players on a house that was more of a luxury hotel than a home for four people, on antiques and artwork that cost ten times more than they would eventually be sold for, on clothing we didn't need, on extravagant vacations, on expensive hobbies like auto racing and helicopter skiing, on outrageously expensive cars, including Ferraris, Bentleys, BMWs, Mercedes, on embarrassing restaurant bills, etc., etc. Without a plan I was a master of consumption, not wealth accumulation.

My lack of career and personal financial planning not only created an unsustainable lifestyle; it also caused me to TOTALLY WASTE my opportunity to realize my share of the value I created by selling enough stock to take care of my family for at least two generations. During my ten years at Cyberonics, I sold approximately 20% of my stock and invested the proceeds in municipal bonds generating some $250,000 per year in tax-free income. I often thought it might be a good idea to sell enough Cyberonics stock to create a municipal bond portfolio generating $1 million per year in tax-free income so I wouldn't have to work and my family's lifestyle wouldn't have to change. When I shared my idea with my then-wife, she proposed that we invest not just in municipal bonds but also in income-producing vacation rentals in Maui or Vail that we knew would be constantly rented and would only appreciate in value. Great ideas, but no plans that were measured, reported, rewarded, and to which we held ourselves accountable.

Unfortunately, without written plans to which to hold you and your life partner—if you have one—accountable, ideas are only ideas . . . great ideas and opportunities of a lifetime that you may ignore or squander. Like I did. In the weeks after Cyberonics received FDA depression approval, and one year before my Cyberonics career, net worth, and reputation were completely destroyed by false options-backdating allegations, I could have sold the 50% of my Cyberonics stock that was vested and freely tradable (my share of the more than $1 billion of value that Cyberonics created for shareholders) for $35 million after taxes, then invested that $35 million in municipal bonds generating $1.5 million per year of tax-free income, and lived happily ever after with or without Cyberonics. Not just me, but my entire family. Including my then-wife, children, and grandchildren. Regardless of what happened to me or my career. In November 2006, my opportunity of a lifetime to realize my share of the value I'd created and take care of my family for generations to come ended. Gone for good. No plan once again equaled opportunities of a lifetime lost.

I wasted a once-in-a-lifetime opportunity that I'd worked for my entire life. All because I didn't do life planning for me and my family and frequently measure, report, and reward the achievement of those plans, just like the business planning that was done by every business with which I was associated, including Cyberonics. Given from whence I came I never dared imagine I would have such an opportunity. Of course I can't imagine a more tragic "woulda, shoulda, coulda" or an event which prompts me to say, "If I knew then what I know now," (or had a confidante with the experience I now have and am sharing with you in this book). One thing I know now for certain is that choosing consumption over the accumulation of income producing assets and investments is a life altering mistake.

Opportunities come in all shapes and sizes and magnitudes. As you think back about personal, professional, romantic, relationship, or financial opportunities that you've had that perhaps you haven't taken full advantage of, ask yourself why. Did you have written personal, professional, and financial plans; intentions and goals on which you were focused, to which you were holding yourself accountable and you were using to make good decisions? Did you regularly update your plans to reflect the knowledge and experience you accumulated each year? If not, why? Is it because, like me, you need(ed) an experienced confidante who has been there, done that, and knows how to maximize your and your family's returns on your significant personal and professional investment?

Perhaps my experience and the expensive lessons I learned can help you. I hope so. Live your intentions through planning. Life planning. Financial planning. Business planning. It's your and your family's life. Opportunities of a lifetime don't come around very often. And they can disappear in the blink of an eye. Trust me, I know. And my former wife and our two children know. Thanks in large part to my failure to effectively do my job as CEO of our family. I repeat, thanks in large part to my failure to effectively do my job as CEO of my life and my family's life.

Before you move on to the next chapter, think about the single biggest personal or professional opportunity you squandered in recent years because you failed to do your job and plan your life and live your plan. What do you wish you'd done differently? One thing I learned the hard way is that opportunities of a lifetime don't come around very often. Squandering them can be very expensive, once-in-a-lifetime lessons. I sure wish I knew then what I know now or had a confidante who did.

Plan your life and live your life plan. Then and only then plan your work and work your plan. What gets thoroughly planned, frequently measured, frequently reported and appropriately rewarded gets done.

CHAPTER 6

BOUNDARIES SET YOU FREE

Boundaries, your personal Declaration of Independence and Bill of Rights, will set you free to create extraordinary relationships and realize your full potential.

A "BOUNDARY," ACCORDING to the *Merriam-Webster Dictionary*, is "something that indicates or fixes a limit or extent." If you own real estate, property lines are the boundaries between your property and your neighbors' properties. There may be boundaries or limits on what you can do with your property if you live in a gated community. Do you drive? If so, things like lines on the road and speed limits are boundaries that provide limits as to where and how you can safely drive. Do you work for a company that has company policies? If so, your employer has boundaries or limits on the company's and employees' behavior to maximize productivity and safeguard the company's mission.

Those are all examples of boundaries created by others and memorialized in writing. They apply equally to everyone. Including you and me. We are expected to know the boundaries/limits that apply to us. Ignorance is not bliss when it comes to boundaries. We of course have a choice as to whether we respect and abide by those boundaries, but authorities, namely the courts, police, homeowners' associations, the human resources department of your company, etc., have a duty to enforce those boundaries/rules when they're broken. The consequences for any of us crossing any of these boundaries are well known. If we violate corporate boundaries, we can lose our jobs. If we don't respect well-known driving boundaries and drive on the wrong side of the road, run red lights, or drive drunk, we can lose a lot more than our jobs.

So what about your personal boundaries? Like property lines and corporate policies, personal boundaries are limits, rules, and principles that define what you consider to be acceptable and unacceptable behavior in your relationships— both your behavior and the behavior of others. Personal boundaries define how you will interact with others and allow others to interact with you. Limit what you will say to others and allow others to say to you. Healthy personal boundaries give you the power to say what, for many, is the most underused word in their vocabulary. "No."

There are many types of personal boundaries, including intellectual, emotional, spiritual, physical, and sexual, to name a few. Personal boundaries define who and what you are, create mutually beneficial relationships of all kinds, enable you to become the master of you from the inside out, and help you create and share the most abundance possible. By creating, communicating, maintaining, enforcing, and living healthy personal boundaries, you are honoring, nurturing, respecting, and loving yourself and telling the world that you are completely comfortable with who and what you are. You are also telling the world that you expect others to respect your boundaries, just as you will respect theirs. Maintaining healthy personal boundaries and respecting others' healthy personal boundaries are key ingredients to living with integrity as defined by "to thine own self be true" and "do unto others as you would have them do unto you."

Just like property lines and corporate policies, to be effective your personal boundaries must be communicated and consistently applied/enforced. One thing that dogs, kids, and adults seem to have in common is that we all seem to like rules, principles, and boundaries consistently applied to everyone equally. Arbitrary communication and enforcement of personal boundaries confuses everyone including ourselves. If you don't create, live, and consistently enforce healthy personal boundaries, what are you telling yourself and the world about your worth and value? That you're not worthy and don't deserve love and respect? If you don't respect the personal boundaries of others with whom you have a relationship, what are you telling them? That they're not as worthy as you and deserve less respect and love than you?

My ongoing self-mastery, awakening, and empowerment journey, starting with my study of tantra, has taught me a lot about the importance of boundaries and what for me constitutes healthy boundaries. Before starting my study of tantra at age fifty-seven, I never much thought about nor did I create healthy personal boundaries. Some things I have since learned are (1) my lack of healthy boundaries were the result of my childhood programming, (2) my lack of healthy boundaries caused me to waste numerous opportunities of a lifetime to create multigenerational abundance and positive, healthy, personal and professional relationships, (3) healthy boundaries come from within, not without, (4) setting, maintaining, and living healthy boundaries that constitute my personal Bill of Rights is essential to me living with integrity and realizing my full potential, and (5) creating, communicating, and enforcing personal boundaries from the inside out is no small task.

So let's have a look at your personal boundaries and Bill of Rights:

- Do you always, frequently, sometimes, or never put others' wants, needs, and feelings ahead of yours? Think about a time when you did so, and write down a description of what happened and why you put yourself second.

- Do you always, frequently, sometimes, or never accommodate or indulge without consequence your significant other's, spouse's, and/or children's inappropriate, disrespectful, or hurtful words or behavior? Think about a time when you did, and write down a description of what happened, why you did what you did, and how it felt.
- Do you always, frequently, sometimes, or never allow others' thoughts, values, opinions, and feelings to define or supersede yours? Think about a time when you did so, and write down a description of what happened, why you did what you did, and how it felt.
- Do you always, frequently, sometimes, or never allow others to infringe on your personal space without being given permission, such as entering a room you're in when the door is closed, hugging you, or touching you intimately or sexually? Think about a time when you did, and write down a description of what happened, why you did what you did, and how it felt.
- Are you afraid to exercise your right to say no? How often do you implicitly or explicitly say yes when you really wanted to say no? Describe in writing a time when you didn't say no, why you didn't, and how not saying no made you feel.
- Do you have separate boundaries for professional relationships, friends of the same and opposite sex, acquaintances, family members, lovers, and those with whom you're intimate? Write down your boundaries with each group.

- How often do you communicate your personal boundaries to those around you and do you consistently enforce those boundaries by speaking up and creating consequences if they're crossed?
- Do you hesitate to create, communicate, and/or enforce your personal boundaries out of fear that you won't be liked or loved or you will destroy a relationship as a result?
- Do you respect others' personal boundaries? Think about a recent situation when you did and did not respect the boundaries of someone very important to you. Why did and didn't you respect those boundaries? What happened and what did you learn?
- Who in your life has what you consider to be the best personal boundaries? What are those boundaries and why do you think they're the best?

Even after all the reading and self-mastery work I've done on boundaries, I feel uncomfortable when I ask myself the same questions I just asked you. When I ask myself why, a couple of things come to mind. First, that my childhood programming taught me that my needs didn't matter, everyone else's wants and needs superseded mine, and that I wasn't entitled to nor deserved any personal boundaries. Second, although I know that personal boundaries will create clarity and certainty and set me free to live the best life with the healthiest relationships possible, I am fearful that they will do the opposite and somehow put me in a metaphorical solitary confinement. Lastly, although I've come a long way in terms of creating, communicating, living, and enforcing healthy personal boundaries and relationships, I still have a long way to go.

Are you like me in that you find it much easier to live by workplace boundaries than personal boundaries? Regardless of whether I was a board member, chairman of the board, CEO, vice president, salaried, or hourly employee, I had no trouble communicating, living by, and enforcing corporate policies— professional boundaries that I in part created or had no part in creating. Not-so-personal boundaries, even though my lack of personal boundaries repeatedly cost me one opportunity of a lifetime after another and destroyed many relationships.

The reasons for my lack of personal boundaries astound me even today. It's obvious to me now that I constantly accepted and never challenged my childhood programming that was clearly not in my or my family's best interests—or, as it turned out, in the best interests of millions of people whose lives were touched by severe treatment-resistant illnesses. My problem wasn't that I honored, respected, abided by, and enforced professional boundaries. It was that I didn't understand the importance of personal boundaries and, until recently, failed to create, communicate, abide by, and enforce healthy personal boundaries.

1. I believed that professional boundaries were more valid and legitimate because they were institutional boundaries based on experienced professionals' years of relevant experience. My personal boundaries were simply my boundaries based only on my limited experience and were therefore illegitimate and invalid.

2. Professional boundaries were memorialized and communicated in writing with every person to whom those boundaries applied and who agreed that they read,

understood, and would abide by those
boundaries. Until recently, I never thought
my personal boundaries were worthy of
being communicated and I believed that it
would be inappropriate for me to ask others
to acknowledge and agree to abide by my
boundaries.

3. I believed that creating, communicating,
    abiding by, and enforcing professional
    boundaries was definitely in the best interest
    of the corporation and every person who had
    a relationship with the corporation. I also
    believed that the enforcement of corporate
    boundaries would enable the corporation and
    every employee to realize their full potential.
    I wasn't convinced until recently that my
    personal boundaries had a similar value and
    were of similar importance to me and anyone
    with whom I had a relationship.

4. I believed that if I didn't abide by and enforce
    professional boundaries, I would lose my
    job and career. Little did I know that by not
    creating, abiding by, and enforcing healthy
    personal boundaries, I could and would (and
    ultimately did) lose my job, career, net worth,
    and an opportunity of a lifetime to create
    multigenerational abundance for my family
    and improve hundreds of thousands if not
    millions of people's lives.

Here are a few examples of how I abided by and enforced
professional boundaries after which I will provide you with

examples of what inadequate personal boundaries cost me and my family:

In today's highly litigious and politically charged world, understanding and adhering to the policies of your employer—especially if you are self-employed—and living within boundaries is essential to protect your career and maximize your success. It's easy. Read the corporate policies and if you have any questions, ask the appropriate person in HR, then regardless of what you, your boss, or your colleagues might think, respect and abide by the corporate policies. Especially if you're a manager.

The consequences for violating corporate policies are well known, so your choice should be an informed one. You know and understand the written policies. You know the consequences for not abiding by those policies. Why in the world would someone choose to knowingly "cross the line"? Why shouldn't the same be true for our personal relationships? Meaning that both people in a relationship know the other's boundaries and the consequences for violating those boundaries.

When I was in the venture capital business and chairman of a company in which the venture capital firm in which I was a general partner was a large investor, the CEO and I were waiting for our table in the bar at a nice restaurant the night before the board meeting. Two of the company's female sales reps came over and said hello. We talked about business and the growth they were forecasting for their accounts. The CEO asked them if they'd like to continue the conversation over dinner. Before they could say yes, I interrupted, told the sales reps that it was nice meeting them, and asked them to excuse us as we had board committee business to discuss. After being seated at our table, I asked the CEO if he wanted the two of us to go out to dinner with all one hundred sales reps in the company. He seemed puzzled that I would ask such a question. I then added that if we had dinner with two female sales reps, we would have to have dinner with every other sales rep to avoid any potential allegations of sexual harassment, wrongful termination, favoritism—claims because of boundaries inconsistently applied. As I explained to the CEO, dinner with the two female sales reps would have been a no-win situation. If their jobs were eliminated or they didn't get the promotion or bonus they expected, they might allege it was because they spurned what they might claim were our inappropriate advances. If they did get promoted, others might say it was because of the "special favors" they did for us after dinner. The lesson being that interpreting company policies and boundaries broadly and applying those policies and boundaries uniformly to everyone in the organization kept everyone "safe."

Another great example of a corporate boundary was the policy regarding reasonable and appropriate personal use of company assets, including computers and mobile phones, at another company where I was a board member. All employees gave the company the right to inspect their computers or phones in the event that unusual activity was identified. All employees were aware of the boundary, how it would be enforced, and the consequences for violating it. In one case, a regional sales manager was showing a couple of sales reps who worked for him some porn on his company computer. One of those sales reps took offense and reported the inappropriate behavior to HR. The next time the regional sales manager was at headquarters, his computer was inspected. The IT department found almost as much porn as he had sales reports and he went home without a job. Apparently he didn't respect the company's policies or his fellow sales rep's personal boundaries. He also apparently didn't understand that boundaries protected the company and all its employees. I wonder what he said to his wife?

In another case, a marketing manager's cellphone bill was

more than $10,000 in one month. Her phone was inspected and the company discovered over $8,000 in psychic hotline charges. She was called into HR—and because she had no idea why she was called in, meaning that she wasted over $8,000 on a non-psychic psychic—she, too, lost her job.

In addition to policies that apply to all employees, the board of directors sets corporate boundaries for the CEO. When I was in the venture capital business and on the board of a start-up company in Dallas, the young CEO proposed that we approve some outrageous amount of money to lease a skybox at Texas Stadium so he could entertain customers during Dallas Cowboys games. Given the outrageous cost and the fact that we didn't yet have a finished product, the board unanimously voted no. A few months later, a temp was opening the mail for the CEO who was out of town. When she saw a past-due invoice from the Dallas Cowboys for a very large amount, she went to the company's founder, who promptly called one of the board members. A full investigation ensued and we discovered that the young CEO spent more than $500,000 of the company's money not only on the Texas Stadium skybox, but also expensive car leases for him and his wife, an expensive aquarium for his office, clothes for him and his wife, and more. In exchange for the board agreeing not to press criminal charges, the young CEO and his wife surrendered to the company all of his stock and the property he bought with company funds. Breaking corporate boundaries and short-term greed didn't pay off for him. Three months after his resignation, we sold the company. His shares would have been worth over $5 million.

Given that corporate policies are designed to protect and help companies and every employee realize their full potential, violating a professional boundary can destroy companies. I was on the board of a relatively early stage but publicly traded company whose vice president of sales believed he would lose his job if the company's sales fell short of Wall Street's expectations for the quarter. As a result, he proposed a Rolex watch bonus for all the sales reps as a special incentive. The CEO rejected the VP's proposal telling him that sales should reflect only real demand for the product, not special sales incentives. The VP ignored the CEO and not only created the Rolex bonus program, but also gave the sales reps almost carte blanche to create whatever sales terms they needed to sell product. The sales reps responded as expected. They wrote some very creative sales terms, the company reported record sales, and every sales rep won a Rolex. Immediately after the quarter ended and results were reported to Wall Street, the company's VP of finance resigned, supposedly for a better offer. The CEO was surprised by the resignation until he received a call a few days later from NASDAQ asking a lot of questions about the resignation, the company's sales for the quarter, and the company's six months of uncollected receivables.

When the CEO asked for the information requested by NASDAQ, he discovered that the VP of finance had no standard sales terms and no credit policies so he in essence enabled the VP of sales and the sales force to do whatever they wanted to earn their Rolexes regardless of company policies and accounting rules. NASDAQ ordered an audit of every sale in the prior year, which the company passed, thanks to the CEO taking personal responsibility for the audit. Had the company failed the audit, it would have likely lost its listing on NASDAQ, gone bankrupt, and been shut down, costing some two hundred people their jobs. So what happened to the VP of sales? The CEO called him in and asked him what he would do if the roles were reversed and the CEO was the insubordinate who put his own and the sales force's best interests above those of the company. The VP of sales responded, "If I was the CEO, I would fire the VP of sales." To which the CEO responded, "Good idea, you're fired."

So now let's move on to the much more challenging subject of personal boundaries. Healthy personal boundaries are at the top of my list when it comes to things I wish I knew then that I know now. Personal boundaries define how you will interact with others and allow others to interact with you. Limit what you will say to others and allow others to say to you. Creating, communicating, living, and enforcing healthy personal boundaries goes hand-in-hand with overcoming your origin challenge, creating and implementing your happiness formula, consistently applying your integrity principle, and planning for and living your life plan to create and share maximum abundance on every level. Personal boundaries apply to all your relationships, with yourself and others. Whatever your personal boundaries, they should help you become the best version of yourself, realize your full potential, create and share abundance, and help you create and maintain the strongest relationships possible.

Boundaries with Your Spouse/Significant Other

One of the major reasons that my marriage of twenty-one years ended in 2017 is that my previous spouse and I didn't create, live, and enforce personal and relationship boundaries. Written boundaries that in essence represented personal and relationship contracts with ourselves and with each other, one of the most important being how we would handle disagreements, hurt feelings, anger, conflict, and discord. Given from whence I came and my parents' constant waging of World War III (third and final marriage to each other and the only one I witnessed) with no apparent boundaries whatsoever, I'm surprised that I didn't see the need for relationship boundaries regarding disagreements with my wife. Although, since I didn't understand from whence

I came and didn't overcome my origin challenge until it was too late for my marriage, I'm really not all that surprised.

I wish my previous wife and mother of my children and I would have created a boundary that required us to table all disagreements, hurt feelings, etc., until we were in private place at a mutually convenient time when we could be calm and fully present in the moment. Implicit in that boundary is no disagreements or arguing that could be heard by our children or anyone else. Implicit in that boundary is that we would not have disagreed or argued in public. Other healthy boundaries that would have facilitated timely and amicable conflict resolution would have been no name calling, no swearing, no raising of voices, no screaming and yelling—which, if they occurred, would end the discussion until cooler heads prevailed and both of us could respect and live within those boundaries.

I also wish we'd had a boundary and agreement on what we would do if we disagreed or argued about the same issue more than twice, including either (a) agreeing to disagree and never bring it up again, or (b) seeking professional help to find a compromise. Lastly I wish we would have had personal boundaries that would not have allowed either of us to bring up anything that we had agreed was in the past and we were finished discussing. Or things for which an apology had been made and accepted and forgiveness granted.

We created no such boundaries and, as a result, we destroyed our marriage by repeatedly over at least the last three years arguing about the same things over and over, increasingly heatedly, including more and more name calling, profanity, yelling, threats of divorce, etc., increasingly within earshot of others, with rapidly growing distrust and disrespect. Not understanding and respecting the significance of from whence I came, I allowed a wonderful marriage to be destroyed by history repeating itself, namely my former wife and I becoming my mother and father. You have to be kidding me. No, Skip, I'm not.

Other personal and spouse/significant other boundaries I wish I/we would have created, lived by, and enforced included healthier boundaries regarding work hours and the use of cellphones and computers at home and working while on family vacations and during family time. In other words, if I knew then what I know now, I would have created and strictly enforced personal boundaries that would have made me more fully present and focused on my marriage, my wife, and my children, thereby producing more abundance, pleasure, and bliss for all of us.

Boundaries with Children

I now know that maintaining healthy boundaries in our relationships with our children is very important when you consider that as parents, we are primarily responsible for much of our children's origin programming and challenges. Knowing what I know now, I look at boundaries in our relationships with our children as the values, morals, ethics, and integrity that we are teaching them. I also see boundaries with our children as teaching them about reciprocity in healthy relationships. That life isn't all about their needs and wants at the expense of others, including their parents. My observation is that the fewer the boundaries in our relationships with our children or the more inconsistent their enforcement, the increased risk that our children will define their own boundaries and become accommodated, indulged, and entitled teenagers and adults. Especially in today's world with social media, celebrities, movies, the internet, etc., providing constant alternative parenting and programming.

Although my former wife and the mother of our two successful young adult children and I had no clue what personal boundaries were, we nonetheless apparently did a reasonably good job applying our "privileges equal responsibilities" and "rules consistently applied" philosophies that essentially represented relationship boundaries with our children. We periodically communicated our daughter's and son's privileges and responsibilities to them in writing to avoid any memory lapses, by them or us, and make enforcement predictable for them and us. We always asked our son and daughter if what we were proposing was fair and, if not, how it needed to be changed. Our daughter and son at times complained that they felt like employees with a corporate policies manual, but both knew what their privileges were, what their responsibilities were, and what the consequences and bonuses would be for successfully over-delivering on or ignoring their responsibilities.

Their responsibilities included always being honest and telling the truth, the whole truth, and nothing but the truth; respecting their parents, teachers, coaches, and all other adults in words and deeds; being polite and well-mannered; being genuinely sorry when appropriate and modifying their behavior accordingly; academic and athletic performance as defined by their past performance; healthy phone and computer use; and healthy social development, meaning developing a network of friends, staying away from drugs and alcohol, and staying out of trouble in school and in general. When they failed to honor their responsibilities, they knew what privileges they would lose and for what length of time—which they had already agreed was fair. The consequences would be modified based on reasonable mitigating circumstances. When they overachieved their goals and responsibilities, they were rewarded with bonuses. Cash, a car, a special trip, summer camp..

Personal Boundaries at Work
My single biggest failure regarding personal boundaries during my time at Cyberonics was my failure to keep professional

relationships completely separate from personal relation-ships, especially with board members, investors, and analysts. Thinking that I had a personal relationship with investors and analysts—based on my "from whence I came" need to be liked—caused me to do some really dumb things with my stock. I sold about 15% of my stock in February 2005 after we received the FDA approvable letter for depression. Although investors buy and sell stock, including 100% of their positions every day, several investors and analysts went crazy and accused me of saying one thing (Cyberonics is a great investment) and doing another (selling stock). Never mind that the trading window for officers opens infrequently. Never mind that Cyberonics stock had been incredibly volatile. Never mind that all investors, including management teams, diversify their portfolios. Believing that I owed investors with whom I had personal relationships an expla-nation, I wrote an email to all investors and analysts explaining why I sold stock. HUGE mistake. By doing so, I reinforced in my own mind that (1) I had personal relationships with investors and analysts who in reality could care less about me person-ally, and (2) I had done something wrong and let them down by selling even a small percentage of my share of the Cyberonics value I created.

So what do you think happened six months later in July 2005 when I could have, and should have, sold all my vested stock after depression approval, put at least $30 million in the bank, and resigned so Cyberonics could hire a CEO without all the enemies I had created? I did none of it because I didn't want to let down my investor and analyst "friends." The same investors and analysts who in late 2006 ganged up on and destroyed me following false options backdating allegations. Why I thought I had personal relationships with people who only cared about money is beyond me.

I also mistakenly thought I had both professional and personal relationships with Cyberonics board members, most of whom had known me for more than a decade and had met my wife and children. As such, I believed that the board had no doubts about my personal and professional integrity, no doubts about my personal and professional commitment to Cyberonics' mission, and no doubts about me personally and professionally and Cyberonics under my leadership strictly complying with all laws and regulations in the best interests of Cyberonics' mission. Just like with investors, I should have known better. When false options backdating allegations triggered an SEC inquiry, an avalanche of negative media stories, and a proxy fight to unseat the board, no board member defended me.

Even worse, after the options inquiry found that Cyberonics had consistently followed the options-granting processes provided by its outside legal counsel and auditors, there was nothing wrong with any of my options and that I did nothing wrong with regard to options, the Cyberonics board denied me all due process before demanding my resignation. Instead of allowing me to read and analyze the options report, giving me a full and fair hearing, then rendering a verdict face-to-face like suspected criminals receive in our legal system, the board had the company's SEC attorney call my attorney with a not-so-veiled threat of SEC action if I didn't resign and significantly compromise on my severance package. SEC action when I did nothing wrong? So much for personal relationships, let alone good-faith professional relationships. Another HUGE mistake on my part.

Phone Boundaries

It appears to me as though cellphones and the lack of healthy phone boundaries are damaging as many relationships as they're enhancing. What's so important that cellphones can't stay out of sight and mind when a couple is having dinner or when kids are having dinner with their friends, parents, or grandparents? My boundary regarding cellphones with my grown children now is that they are out of sight during family time, which includes at least meals. Just when I think I finally have full compliance, I make the mistake of checking something on my phone relevant to our conversation or plans for the next day. After that, forget it. The phones come out and the conversation now includes the four or five friends they're texting, Snapchatting, on Instagram with. As a result, I've stopped bringing my phone to meals.

Do you "sleep" with your phone? Do you take your phone out to dinner? Are you having an affair with your phone? Do you text or talk more on your phone? Do you have texting boundaries? Are your texting boundaries different than your talking boundaries? If your phone is always out and/or you're always looking at it, what do you think you're saying about the people you're with, including your significant other/spouse, children, parents, friends? Do you think you're telling them that they're important and that you respect their boundaries?

My personal cellphone boundary was much more successful at Cyberonics. At work do you have cellphone rules? At Cyberonics, if you were in a meeting with the CEO, namely me, your phone was either "checked at the door" or turned off. Including mine. My policy was consistently communicated at the start of every meeting. I abided by my own policy. Every thirty minutes to an hour, breaks were provided so that everyone in attendance could attend to "phone matters" without disrupting the flow of the meeting. Anyone who had a potential personal or professional emergency to attend to during the meeting disclosed that potential emergency and was allowed to have their phone on vibrate to step out of the meeting and take their emergency call if it came in. Depending on the timing of the call and who received it, we would all take a break at the same time. If I started looking at my phone or others were allowed to look at their phones without being reminded of the phone rules, then the "flexible phone boundaries" would communicate to everyone in the meeting that whatever was on their prone was more important than our meeting. Makes sense doesn't it? Why have a meeting and require certain people to attend if the subject matter isn't sufficiently important to require everyone's undivided attention?

As you might guess from previous chapters, I'm only now creating personal and relationship boundaries that improve the quality of my life and the lives of those with whom I have relationships, including myself. The limited boundaries I previously had were a reflection of from whence I came in terms of fear of abandonment; nonstop giving; my reliance on me, myself, and I; and a feeling that I'm responsible for satisfying the wants and needs of everyone around me. Meaning that whatever my boundaries were, they were flexible and regularly being compromised to satisfy what I perceived to be the more important wants, needs, demands, and boundaries of my spouse/significant other, my children, friends, or Cyberonics.

Are you like I used to be in that your boundaries aren't consistently communicated and enforced? How do you feel when you compromise your boundaries and allow others to cross them? How do you feel when you say yes even though you want to say no? Does having flexible boundaries serve you or those with whom you have relationships? If your boundaries are flexible and situational, are you predictable? Easy to deal with? Are you living life from a perspective of abundance or lacking? In other words, does your life lack significance and importance such that you must always compromise who and what you are, your boundaries, and "rules of the road" just to please others? If that's the case, think about the affect you may be having on your relationships and those with whom you have a relationship. Are you creating relationships based on reciprocity and mutual trust or respect? Or are you creating accommodated, indulged, and entitled relationship partners who have no interest in reciprocity?

As you now think about your personal and professional boundaries and contemplate the questions at the beginning of the chapter, can you think of at least one relationship that could be significantly improved with better boundaries? If so, create, communicate, live, and enforce a set of personal boundaries that work for both you and your relationship partner and see what happens. If the person with whom you have a relationship truly values your relationship, the relationship will improve. If they don't, they probably won't respect your boundaries and the relationship will end. In either case, you're better off.

CHAPTER 7

COMMON LANGUAGE, VOCABULARY, AND EXPERIENCE CREATES EFFECTIVE COMMUNICATION

Even if we speak the same language and use words as defined in the same dictionary, can we really communicate without common experience?

YOU HEAR SOMEONE on the street say, "Trump is an ass-hole." Do you agree or disagree? Regardless of whether you agree or disagree, do you know which Trump the person is referring to? Do you know what definition of ass-hole is being used by that person? Do you know what your definition of ass-hole is? Do you know whether your definition of ass-hole is the same as the person who made the statement? Are you aware of the person's experience that provides the context for the statement? Do you know which Trump the person is referring to? Do you know whether you and the person who make the statement share common experience with the same Trump that the speaker is referring to?

What if the person who made the statement considered the term *ass-hole* to be a compliment because they believe that in order to deal effectively with Democrats in Congress, a Republican president needs to be an ass-hole? What if the person who made the statement had prior business dealings with whichever Trump he or she was referring to and lost money, thereby justifying calling the Trump they dealt with an ass-hole?

Based on your answers to my previous questions, did you effectively communicate or miscommunicate with the stranger on the street by agreeing or disagreeing?

According to the *Oxford English Dictionary*, communication is "the imparting or exchanging of information by speaking, writing, or using some other medium." Implicit in this definition is that for communication to be effective, the person receiving it must understand what's being communicated. Sounds like Dr. Seussian logic, but it's not. As evidenced by the above hypothetical, effective communication is not as easy as we might think. Let's together make a list of all the requirements in order for us to communicate effectively with someone:

1. Speaking the same language. Not easy, considering how many different versions of English there are and how much slang is now considered acceptable.

2. Using words for which we have the same definition. Not easy considering how many different dictionaries there are, from *Merriam-Webster* to *Oxford* to the *Urban Dictionary*. Take the word "dope," for instance. Is your definition of dope the same as someone twenty years your junior or senior?

3. Is the receiver of the information listening to (or reading) what the imparter of the information has said/written? Not easy for all

the obvious reasons, not the least of which are mobile phones.

4. Both the imparter and receiver must share common experience to put the words in an experiential context so that what is being communicated is truly understood. This can prove extremely difficult. We all have different experiences that provide unique experiential definitions for words and phrases we say, write, read, and hear.

5. A willingness on both the imparter's and receiver's part to ask for and provide clarification. Not easy considering that people don't like to admit what they don't know and repeatedly ask, "What do you mean by that?"

6. Other requirements? You decide.

Looking at our list of requirements for effective communication, do you think you communicate effectively or miscommunicate more often than not? Here's an exercise to help you evaluate the effectiveness of your recent communications:

- Make a list of three recent instances, outside of a work or professional environment, in which you were the imparter of information that, upon reflection, was ineffectively communicated. List which effective communication requirements were not met that caused the communications to be ineffective. In each case, write down what you could have done differently to make the communication more effective.

- Do the same for three instances when you were the

recipient of information that, upon reflection, was ineffectively communicated.

- Do the same for three instances in a business or professional setting when information you imparted was, upon reflection, ineffectively communicated.
- Do the same for three professional/work communications in which you received information that was ineffectively communicated.
- Think about and make a list of three interviews in which a public figure, like a politician, professional athlete, celebrity, or expert communicated something that you assumed you understood but, upon reflection, realized you didn't. What conclusions did you jump to and why?
- Make of a list of three recent times when you asked an imparter of information what they meant when they used a certain word or when they said or wrote something—whether it be in a text, email, or other written form. Make a second list of three instances when you didn't ask someone what they meant and assumed that you knew. Make sure you include texts and emails, which are the breeding ground of troublesome gross miscommunication. Did you really understand what the person meant in both cases? Such as someone who told you another person was spiritual or a narcissist or a Nazi or a racist? Or someone described something they saw or did as breathtaking or dope? Or someone told you that someone did something that triggered them?

I came to appreciate the inherent weaknesses of word-based knowledge and the incredible strengths of experience-based knowledge while studying tantra. It's one thing to be told about the effect of breathing and sounding on your energies. It's considerably more powerful to actually feel the effects of various breathing and sounding techniques on your energies, especially the movement of energies throughout your body.

Word-based knowledge is something we acquire by listening to or reading words. We acquire experiential knowledge when our senses experience something. Living and experiencing are considerably more powerful than simply reading and hearing words. Experiential knowledge turns 2-D black-and-white words into a 3-D brilliant, multicolored feast for all your senses. Think about something you experienced that was "awesome." Bungee jumping. Seeing a grizzly bear in the wild. Playing a piano piece almost perfectly. Experiencing complete bliss with your spouse. Can you describe in words the "awesome" you experienced to someone who never experienced the same thing and have them fully comprehend your experience? Unlikely. Therein lies the power of experiential knowledge and the importance of common experience to effective communication.

I joined Continental Illinois Venture Corporation and became a venture capitalist in 1981. At the time, I had no experience whatsoever. I had no comprehension of what a venture capitalist was. When I'd meet people and they'd ask me what I did, I would replay, "I'm a venture capitalist at Continental Bank." They would nod their heads knowingly as if they knew what a venture capitalist was, even though in most cases they had no clue. Seldom would I ever get the question, "What in the world is a venture capitalist and what exactly do you do?" Probably because the person I'd just met didn't want to appear to be dumb, or unbeknownst to them, was as inexperienced and as uninformed as me! Given that there was common experience in our case, namely none, I suppose we had as much real communication as we could. Specifically very limited word-based communication in which we didn't even have common definitions for the words we were using.

One of the first things I was told in the venture capital business was that the three most important determinants of a start-up or early stage company's success are management, management, management. Meaning, of course, experience, experience, experience of management. My reactions to what I was told were reflections of my "from whence I came" reliance on me, myself, and I, and my complete lack of venture capital experience. Both reactions also confirmed that I had no real experiential understanding of what I was being told. My first reaction was to discount the importance of experience and think that, in my case, I could make up for my lack of venture capital experience by working hard and being smart. My second reaction was to ass-u-me that I understood what I was being told and that I knew how to evaluate management by reading their business plan, comparing their résumés to what they were trying to do in the new company, and asking them penetrating questions. As Jethro from *The Beverly Hillbillies* might have said if he were me, "Uncle Jed, I be a venture capitalist so let's commence to go evaluate us some management."

Late in the afternoon on my first Friday, John Hines, the president of Continental Illinois Venture Corp. and a legend in the venture capital business, who made hundreds of millions of dollars for Continental Bank in Chicago, stopped by my cubicle. We chatted about my first week and then he gave me a stack of roughly ten business plans to review over the weekend and be prepared to present at our Monday morning meeting. I felt honored that John would come down to my cubicle and ask me to review business plans. Little did I know that venture capital school was about to begin!

Over the weekend, I read most of the business plans cover to cover and took notes on what I thought were their strengths and weaknesses and what we should do next. The summary of one plan for antigravity boots was so ridiculous that I didn't bother to read past the product description.

The Monday morning meeting started promptly at 8 a.m. All investment professionals were in attendance, including John, four vice presidents, and two associates. Nobody other than me had less than two years' experience. New investment opportunities and existing portfolio companies were discussed at the meeting. To say that John Hines was rather direct is a gross understatement. Almost immediately after the meeting began, John looked at me and asked, "How was your weekend, Cummins? Did you read those business plans I gave you?" Before I could even say yes, he asked me, "What did you think of the antigravity boot business plan, specifically the management team?"

Not yet comprehending the lesson I was about to be taught regarding experience, or that I probably wasn't the first rookie to be given the anti-gravity boot business plan, I confidently responded, "Well, John, the product seemed so silly that I didn't bother reading anything other than the summary."

John leaned back in his chair, put his feet up on his desk and lit his pipe. He then looked at each of the vice presidents and raised his eyebrows before locking on to me and beginning his Spanish Inquisition lesson on venture capital. "Mind if I ask you a few questions, Cummins?" John asked. John's machine-gun questions, followed by my one- or two-word answers, came rapid fire:

"How long have you been in the venture capital business, Cummins?"

"Less than a week . . . ."

"How many venture capital investments have you ever made, Cummins?"

"None."

"How much money have you made investing in start-up or early stage companies, Cummins?"

"None."

"How many years' experience in venture capital do I have, Cummins?

"Over twenty."

"Did I ask you to read all the business plans I gave you on Friday afternoon?"

"Yes."

"So why didn't you do what I asked and be prepared to talk about management for every one of those companies? You know that management is by far the most important factor in our investment decisions, don't you?

"I made a mistake."

"Did you sleep this weekend, Cummins?"

"Well, yes."

"Then do me a favor, SLEEP LESS!"

Having learned experientially the importance of experience and management in the John Hines School of Venture Capital, I still needed to be taught how to properly evaluate management. That class began a week or so later when I went out by myself to meet with a start-up company seeking venture capital. In Silicon Valley no less, the epicenter of venture capital. I spent about four hours at the company, first meeting with the management team as a group, then meeting individually with each of the three vice presidents and an hour with the CEO. I thought I was well prepared for the meeting. I had a long list of questions about the product that was still under development, technology risks, market, competition, financing needs, projections, and each of the vice presidents' and the CEO's backgrounds. I really liked the people and what I heard, so I returned to Chicago on Friday morning looking forward to the next Monday morning meeting at which I would present my recommendation that we move forward with due diligence.

About halfway through the Monday meeting, John asked me what I thought about the company and its management team. This time I was ready! Or so I thought. I pulled out my notes, gave a quick summary of the investment opportunity, then began providing details of the management team's impressive backgrounds. Once I finished my overview of the CEO's background, with John nodding his head in apparent approval, he once again started asking a lot of questions to find out what I really knew about the CEO and—as I now know—from whence the CEO came. Was the CEO married? Divorced? How long was he married? Any kids? What sports did he like? Did he play sports in high school or college? What are his hobbies? Where does he like to go on vacation? How often does he take vacations? Where did he grow up? What did his parents do for a living? What does he regret most? If he could do one thing differently, what would it be? What didn't he like about his previous job? What's his salary history? What kind of car does he drive? How big of a house does he live in? Etc., etc. Of course I didn't have answers to these very important questions, but this time John wasn't so hard on me. His obvious point made, he ended Lesson #2 in the John Hines School of Venture Capital by telling me, "Call the CEO and see when you can go back out and meet with him, then come see me and I'll teach you how to properly evaluate management."

I did exactly as John suggested and went back out to meet with the CEO, but this time we met briefly at the company then went to his home, changed, went for a run (he was unfortunately a marathon runner), then showered, had cocktails at his house followed by dinner at a restaurant of his choice. All told I spent about six hours with the CEO really getting to know him personally, including from whence he came. It was a triple win. I learned everything about the CEO and then some. The CEO and I also now had more common experience to facilitate more effective future communications. Lastly, I acquired invaluable experiential knowledge about myself and how to effectively evaluate management.

As I write this, I recall similar coaching that I received during my CIA interviews from a previous case officer who had worked in the Soviet Union for many years. He asked me what I would do if I wanted to develop a relationship with a Soviet official. I responded by saying that I would invite the Soviet official to go do some sort of activity, like play golf. The former case officer laughed out loud, complimented me on my activity idea, then told me that the only Soviet officials who play golf are KGB officers trying to develop relationships with Americans. I then said, "Okay, no golf, how about fishing?" to which my CIA interviewer replied, "Now you're talking, they all love fishing." The consistent messages from both John Hines and the CIA being that in order to really know someone, you must know them personally, including from whence they came, which doesn't happen sitting in an office or conference room.

Note that as with the personal boundaries mentioned in the previous chapter, neither John Hines nor the CIA recommended that I relax my personal boundaries and develop a personal relationship with the CEO or Soviet official like I mistakenly did with the Cyberonics board. Rather, they were teaching me how to cultivate relationships with appropriate boundaries which were aligned with my purposes for those relationships.

Interviewing and communications with a relatively new person at Cyberonics was predictably tricky given that without common experience, there is no real communication—and we were pioneering new hybrid drug and device ways of doing things. The most difficult communication being in sales and marketing. With epilepsy, our sales and marketing goal was to create awareness, acceptance, and demand for our unique device-based therapy among neurologists, nurses, hospitals, surgeons, insurance companies, and patients and their families. That's six different customers, almost all of which had never considered using any treatment other than a drug.

So who should we hire? Sales and marketing people with device experience who had only ever sold and marketed devices, such as pacemakers to cardiologists and hospitals to treat cardiac patients? Or drug people who had sold and marketed antiepileptic drugs to neurologists but had no clue how to sell and market a device? Or nurse clinical specialists who knew how to educate nurses and patients on a variety of new therapies? We started with device people who had sold and marketed other active implantable devices, such as pacemakers and pain stimulators, but quickly changed our interviewing techniques to focus not so much on device-versus-drug but more on whether they had demonstrated an ability to sell a variety of products using new sales models and processes. We also created an entirely new sales and marketing model that used the experience of device people, drug people, and nurses to focus on creating awareness, acceptance, and demand among all customers, patient by patient. Performance was measured by how effectively qualified patients were moved through a six-step funnel in each prescriber's (neurologist's) practice. Of course we tracked unit and dollar sales by territory—the desired outputs, but more importantly, we tracked each sales and marketing person's "inputs" to create awareness, acceptance and demand for our product primarily among prescribing neurologists, nurses, surgeons and hospitals, and patients and their families as measured by patient funnel yields at each prescriber.

Needless to say, our device sales and marketing team weren't too thrilled with our new sales and marketing model that required them to sell and market a new Cyberonics way, not the traditional device way. Not by themselves but partnered with a nurse clinical specialist. To create common experience and maximize communication, we began measuring and rewarding performance defined not only by sales but also by a variety of inputs including calls on target doctors, patient education events, patients educated, nurses and physicians educated, prior authorizations, physicians participating in the registry, and patients in the registry, all of which drove sales.

To give sales managers a common understanding and experience in addition to word-based knowledge managing inputs as opposed to outputs, we took the sales managers to race-car driving school for Cyberonics' version of the John Hines School of Venture Capital. Over those three days, the driving instructors first limited their coaching to the desired output by telling the sales managers to go faster. Of course, the sales managers only went slower because they had no real idea how to go faster, meaning the inputs they needed to change to go faster. Then the driving instructors turned on the cars' data acquisition systems that measured each of the sales managers' inputs: throttle, brakes, steering, etc., everywhere on the track. After every few laps, the sales managers would come in and get individual coaching on the two inputs their driving instructors were confident they could change that would have the biggest effect on their desired output, which was faster lap times.

As the managers improved their inputs and their lap times improved, their attention was turned to other inputs they could improve to further reduce their lap times. They *all* steadily reduced their lap times. How? By focusing on going faster, namely selling more? Nope. By focusing on the inputs that their coach and the data said would result in them lowering their lap times/ selling more. Racing school provided a common experience for the sales managers that put them on the same page in terms of communicating and coaching inputs, the end result being significantly more consistent and improved sales performance.

What have you done to create common experiences and effective communication with those you work with? Common experiences beget improved communication. Better communication begets improved performance. Better performance as defined by those above you begets promotions and raises.

In terms of personal relationships, what's more important than effective communication? If effective communication is the foundation upon which healthy mutually beneficial personal relationships are built, isn't the onus on each of us, including you and me, to check as many of the effective-communication-requirement boxes as possible? Meaning make sure that we and those we're communicating with, including our spouse or significant other, children, other family members, friends, are as frequently as possible speaking the same language, using a common vocabulary, relying on common experiential knowledge, and asking what is meant when appropriate.

I wish I knew then what I know now regarding communication in personal relationships when it came to my second marriage to the mother of my children. We didn't share a common first language. Hers was Latvian, mine was American English. We often didn't share common definitions of words we were using. We had completely different experiential knowledge regarding our origin challenges, respective happiness formulas, integrity principles, life plans, and personal boundaries. We didn't share common experiential knowledge when it came to raising kids, what constitutes cheating/affairs, budgets, spending, expense sharing, wealth accumulation, etc. And we seldom asked each other the all-important clarifying question, "What do you mean by that?" before jumping to conclusions. Needless to say, our miscommunications created disagreements, which created more miscommunications, and so on.

Had we recognized our challenges with effective communication, we could have at least compensated for our lack of common experience by being more diligent in asking what was meant and agreeing on the definitions of words we were using. Obviously talking louder like the other was hard of hearing didn't improve communication. Whenever we didn't really understand what the other was saying or we felt ourselves jumping to a negative conclusion about what the other was saying, I wish we had taken a deep breath and simply done one or more of the following:

- Said in a non-threatening calm way, "I don't understand what you're saying. Please tell you what you mean."
- Thought about the most positive interpretation for what the other was saying and ask the other if that's what they meant.
- Asked, "What makes you say that?" to better understand what experience/experiential knowledge was behind the other's words.

Had we made those changes, I believe that our miscommunication would have been minimized and I think there's a good chance I would still be happily married today. There are easy changes for you to make in your personal relationship communications before it's too late.

Before I give you your communication challenge, allow me to say something about all the name-calling and use of labels that runs rampant in our society today. Here are a few of the more commonly used labels: fascist, Nazi, racist, misogynist, contro-versial, narcissist, globalist, predator, scumbag, socialist. Think about the ass-hole example at the beginning of this chapter. Do you think that the endless list of names and labels used everyday satisfy any of your effective communication requirements? If not, just say no to labels and name-calling.

So here's my compassionate accountability challenge for you regarding effective communication. Be more conscious of your communication going forward. In all communication, whether it be verbal or written in memos, letters, emails, and texts—especially in emails and texts—be cognizant of whether you're speaking and hearing the same language, whether you have the same definitions of the words being used, and whether you have the same experiential knowledge that puts the words being used and what's being said and heard in the same expe-riential context. Lastly and most important, ask and answer the "What do you mean?" and "What makes you say that?" questions whenever you're not 100% certain that what you're saying is being completely understood or you don't completely understand what's being said. Especially when it comes to texts and emails in which we all say things that we probably wouldn't say to someone's face, and therefore are ripe for damaging miscommunication. Your heightened diligence and consciousness regarding the imparting and receiving of information—communication—will likely improve all your relationships.

And accelerate the mastering of you from the inside out.

CHAPTER 8

THE STATUS QUO CONUNDRUM

To change, or not to change, as in one or more of your status quos.
That is the conundrum.

NOW BEING MORE cognizant of my effective communication requirements, and becoming more of a master of me from the inside out, I feel obliged to tell you that a status quo is "an existing state of affairs" and a conundrum is "a confusing and difficult problem or question." Whether changing a status quo is a good idea has been a conundrum (someone once said that if you use a new word three times it's yours) for centuries.

The presence of status quos and the challenges of changing them have long been a subject of much thought and discussion. In seventh-grade speech class, I had to memorize and recite Hamlet's famous "To be or not to be" soliloquy written in 1599 by William Shakespeare. The most common interpretation of the soliloquy is that Hamlet is considering the conundrum of life versus death. Another interpretation, especially of the beginning of his soliloquy, is that he is debating whether he should change a status quo (hence the subtitle of this chapter):

To be, or not to be; that is the question:
Whether 'tis nobler in the mind to suffer
The slings and arrows of outrageous fortune,
Or to take arms against a sea of troubles,
And, by opposing, end them. . . .

In 1686 Sir Isaac Newton published his famous three laws, the first of which was, "An object at rest stays at rest and an object in motion stays in motion with the same speed and in the same direction unless acted upon by an unbalanced or superior force." He was discussing his laws of physics but could have just as easily been describing the laws of status quos.In his famous political treatise *The Prince*, published in 1532, Machiavelli had a thing or two to say about the difficulties and risks associated with changing status quos when he wrote:

"It must be considered that there is nothing more difficult to carry out nor more doubtful of success nor more dangerous to handle than to initiate a new order of things; for the reformer has enemies in all those who profit by the old order, and only lukewarm defenders in all those who would profit by the new order. This lukewarmness arising partly from the disbelief of mankind who does not truly believe in anything new until they actually have experience of it."

Have you found it difficult to make changes in your life, in the organization you work for, in the world around you? Have you noticed that those status quos that are the most profitable or in which powerful people have a vested interest are the most difficult to change? How have you convinced yourself or others that the change you're trying to make is worth it and will provide even more benefits than the old way?

Let's consider how successfully you've changed status quos.

- Make a list of two changes you've successfully made in your personal life (personal status quos) in the last couple of years. Changes in relationships, boundaries, where you live, the car you drive, nutrition, hobbies, etc. Who was in favor of the change and who was against the change? What were the risks if the change ended up being for the worse? What did you and others have to gain from the change? What was the result?
- Do the same for two changes you unsuccessfully tried to make in your personal life in the last couple of years. Write down why you weren't successful in changing that particular personal status quo.
- Do the same for three changes you successfully made professionally in the last couple of years. Changed jobs, changed companies, started your own company. Changed careers. Went back to school. Reorganized your department. Changed people in your organization. Developed a new product or process, etc.
- Do the same for three changes you've unsuccessfully tried to make in your professional life.
- Make a list of two changes you want to make in your personal life in the next year. Write down what you stand to gain if you're successful and what you stand lose if you're not. Make a list of those people who will support your proposed change and those who will be opposed and what each of those people stand to gain or lose. Given all that you now know about your planned changes in your personal status quos, create a written plan to maximize the probability of your success.

- Make a similar list and do the same for two changes you want to make in your professional life in the next year.

A pointed example of how difficult it is to change a personal status quo is my ongoing twelve-year journey to adjust my life-style and spending so that I'm cash-flow positive on a monthly and yearly basis after becoming unemployed, a 75% drop in my income, an increase in interest rates, and my divorce in 2017.

In this case, I was not only the reformer Machiavelli refers to, but also the enemy who I mistakenly perceived as profiting from the "old order" and the "lukewarm defender" who didn't believe he would profit from the "new order." Before my income dropped, I mistakenly thought that I didn't have to worry about a family budget. The sky was the limit, or so I thought. We didn't have to choose between nice houses, cars, clothes, nice vacations, private sports coaches for our kids, expensive private schools, extravagant hobbies, such as race car driving, helicopter skiing, etc., to be cash-flow positive.

Once my income dropped by over 50% when I left Cyberonics, we adjusted our lifestyle by first largely eliminating the expensive hobbies, downsizing houses and cars, and ending purchases of expensive clothes and jewelry. We also significantly reduced our spending on vacations.

But it wasn't enough, one of the reasons being that I had a line of credit secured by my municipal bonds and stocks at an incredible low floating interest rate of around 1% a year. The other being that I had a huge vested interest in preserving what I mistakenly believed was a lifestyle that defined who I was. When we moved back to Texas in 2009 from a very expensive rented house in Medina, Washington, near where Bill Gates lives, it was as if we were going back to our Texas status quo, of course without the income. I bought a big house, namely 7,500 square feet for three people and two dogs, which we all agreed felt like "home." Unfortunately, while we could afford to buy the house because of my almost-free line of credit, we couldn't afford to live there due to excessive needed improvements, high property taxes, outrageous utilities, air-conditioning, pool maintenance on a hotel-size pool with a water slide, etc., all of which created negative cash flow. We lived in the house for five years and were never cash-flow positive. As a matter of fact, living in that house cost me 20% of my net worth. All because I thought that the status quo of living in an excessively large house provided more emotional and ego "profit" than would appropriately downsizing to a more reasonably sized house that would create positive cash flow. My emotional vested interest in a lifestyle status quo made me the enemy of a change that was clearly in our best interests.

In 2015, during a marital separation, I leased a really nice 1,100-square-foot one-bedroom apartment for $1,200 a month. The combination of that experience, plus what it cost my family of three to live in a 7,500 square-foot-house provided me new rules regarding housing to be cash flow positive. Specifically, the first "resident" would be allocated 1,100 square feet with each subsequent "resident" allocated 600 square feet. Had these new housing rules been applied to the house we bought in 2009, we would have bought a 2,300 square foot house for 65% less and we would have been cash-flow positive after paying taxes, utilities, etc. I would have saved $2 million and that savings invested in tax-free municipal bonds would have generated $80,000 per year starting in 2010 and continuing today.

One thing I definitely wish I knew then that I know now is that it's a lot easier to create a lifestyle and spending status quo than it is to downsize/change one. Just because banks and finance companies will finance ninety to one hundred percent of the purchase price of a new house or car and make us think we can afford to buy it doesn't mean we can afford to own it. Fixed assets like houses and cars come with a lot of fixed expenses, such as loan payments, property taxes, insurance, utilities, maintenance and repairs. And those fixed assets with all their fixed expenses are considerably harder to sell than they are to buy. Remember the real estate crash of 2008?

Changing our lifestyle and spending status quos is something we'll all have to do, given that income doesn't keep increasing forever. Or, in my case, drops precipitously! Before you are forced to reduce spending, invest your savings in income-producing assets to diversify your income to protect yourself if your job disappears. When you reach that point of having to reduce spending, make yourself more than a lukewarm advocate for change by first and foremost not allowing your possessions or lifestyle to define you, then by creating a detailed budget with the goal of maximizing positive cash flow for travel, hobbies, etc., instead of pouring your money into a big house and expensive cars. And consider abandoning the status-quo concept that you must own your home. My experience buying and selling more than my share of houses is that if you can often rent a nice house at a lower after-tax monthly cost than owning. Don't forget that the total cost of home ownership includes monthly mortgage payments, real estate taxes, utilities, the opportunity cost of investing the down payment in dividend-paying stocks or bonds, and the profit or loss you incur when you sell the house net of 6% real estate commissions!

Before moving to Las Vegas, I went through the lease-versus-buy decision in Southern California, ironically just after I first wrote this chapter. Although "just because you can afford to buy doesn't mean you can afford to own" was ringing in my ears, my then significant other, who had lived in Southern California for nineteen years and still had two teenagers there, really wanted to buy a house instead of "throwing our money away on a lease." We anticipated staying in California at most another three years. We found some really nice houses and had a commitment for an interest-only, 10/1 adjustable rate mortgage at 3.75% with 20% down. But when we analyzed the total cost of home ownership versus both of us continuing to lease, the house would have to appreciate over 18% in three years in order for home ownership to be less expensive. If the house's value went sideways from its already mind-blowing $550-per-square-foot price, we would lose over $200,000 when and *if* we sold it. Remember the real estate crash of 2008? Almost everyone in Southern California does except perhaps real estate agents. I'm proud to say that I'm now living in Las Vegas in a house that I not only could afford to buy, but also can afford to own. And I'm finally cash-flow positive! Changing my previous lifestyle and spending status quos only took me thirteen years and cost me several million dollars! If I only knew then what I know now or had read a book like this ten years ago.

Some of the other most difficult personal status quos to change seem to be those associated with social mores, personal philosophies, and/or beliefs. Mores are the customs, conventions, behaviors, norms, and habits of a society or community. These one-size-fits-all status quos probably don't always work for us, but making decisions contrary to them and/or ignoring them can be perceived as being very risky. When I was in the venture capital business, we used to joke, "If we're going to be dumb, let's at least be dumb with smart people." Meaning that it was less risky to invest with other big-name funds than it was to invest solo and be the only dumb one if the investment didn't work. That seems to be true for many of us in our personal lives. We ignore the opportunity to be the really smart one by going it alone and not following the herd because of fear of being perceived as the only dumb one.

Think about all the status quos when it comes to our children's education. When I was a chairman and CEO and lived in Houston, all the best and brightest kids went to certain private schools, all started school as soon as possible regardless of their age and maturity, and all took as many AP (advanced placement) classes as they could. If you ignored those status quos and did something different, your kid obviously wasn't one of the best and brightest. Fortunately my former wife and I figured out that these status quos weren't always in the best interest of our kids and we created new status quos for their education.

Our daughter was taking all AP classes at one of the top private schools in Houston and was obviously overloaded in her junior year. When I asked her why she was taking so many AP classes, she said she was doing so to get college credits so she could graduate from college early and because that's what all the smart kids were doing. She changed her mind and "down-leveled" (think about the implication of that term) into a couple of standard, non-AP classes after I convinced her that college for me was so much fun, there's no way I would have wanted to graduate even one second early and that perhaps the smartest kids weren't taking all-AP classes because they wanted to get the highest grades possible to maximize their chances of getting into their first choice of colleges. Indeed this new status quo worked for her, considering she was accepted early decision and graduated from Dartmouth with a BA in math. Then after working for a couple of years and finding her passion, she was accepted to and graduated from Texas A&M veterinary school with a **Doctor of Veterinary Medicine**.

We created a new status quo for our son as well. Complying with the smart-kids-start-school-early status quo, we made the mistake of enrolling him in pre-K at one of the top private schools in Houston when he was a year younger than most of the other enrollees. Although he was doing very well academically, athletically, and socially, we allowed him to repeat his freshman year in high school so he could realize his dream of playing major college football and be as prepared as possible academically, athletically, and socially to realize his full potential in college. Once again, changing the status quo for our son seems to have worked. Today he is a successful full-scholarship football player at the University of Texas in Austin. Hook 'em Horns!

Another personal status quo that many should consider changing is the idea that people in committed monogamous relationships should be married. Why? If you love each other, have an agreement on kids, what constitutes monogamy and cheating, and have an agreement on expense sharing and distribution of assets when and if your relationship ends, why get married? Why do you need a legal contract that creates an unnecessary presumption of privileges and responsibilities?

Changing status quos can indeed be very difficult, especially when you are the "keepers" of the status quo you need to change. Can you think of a personal status quo you wish you changed a lot earlier than you did? Who were your lukewarm supporters and who were your enemies trying to preserve the status quo? Which were you?

Changing status quos at work can be even more challenging and dangerous. At Cyberonics, I used to ask people all the time why they were doing something a certain way. The answer I would typically get—until everyone figured out how I would react—was, "Because we've always done it this way." Changing people's status quos in terms of how they did their jobs was a major challenge, especially when it involved vice presidents. We hired four vice presidents who had never worked in a start-up, only large companies. They knew one way of doing things: the way that made them successful in the big drug or device company for which they worked previously. When they were challenged to change the way they did things, they weren't happy. They resented the person who was trying to change their status quo, namely me.

The relative difficulty of changing status quos is directly related to the amount of "profits" provided by those status quos to their "keepers." Especially if the "keepers" are "powers that be." In terms of markets, nobody really cared much about the epilepsy market, so changing that status quo for the benefit of patients was relatively easy compared to the depression market. The depression market was ten times the size of the epilepsy market, so the "profits" being realized were considerably larger and the companies and individuals realizing them were considerably larger and much more powerful. I recently read that a cannabinoid (cannabis-based drug) was FDA approved for certain forms of severe juvenile epilepsy. What do you think will happen when such a drug is proposed for depression? The CEO of the company that tries to commercialize such a treatment will probably end up out of a job and career and writing a book, like me.

In 2008, I became the CEO of a start-up that was founded by one of the former vice presidents at Cyberonics, called Generic Medical Devices, or GMD. As indicated by its name, GMD's business plan was to develop, manufacture, and sell fully equivalent, simple, standard-of-care devices at prices 50% below those of the market leaders. The company's first product was an FDA-approved female stress urinary incontinence sling developed in collaboration with a nationally renowned urologist at the Cleveland Clinic. Comprehensive testing demonstrated GMD's product was fully equivalent to the products of the market leaders, except for price. GMD's pricing offered hospitals savings of up to $250,000 per year.

We saw no reason why we wouldn't be successful. We would save hospitals a lot of money and the only thing anyone had to change was the product they were buying and using. No change in surgical procedure, no change in patient outcomes, no change in coverage and reimbursement. Our product was so equivalent that we eventually lost a method patent infringement suit that put GMD out of business. Before that we were struggling to convince hospitals to convert to our product and save money. Why? Because doctors in essence told us, "There's nothing in this for me. What do I get for switching?"

I even had one well-known urologist and consultant for Johnson & Johnson—one of the market leaders—tell me during a visit to his practice that our product was absolutely equivalent, and if he owned an ambulatory surgery center and could personally realize the savings, he would switch immediately. However, he went on to tell me that if he switched while working at the hospital, he wouldn't personally receive any of the hospital's $150,000 in annual savings. Instead he would probably lose all the consulting fees he was being paid by Johnson & Johnson, which wouldn't make his wife happy because his wife liked "nice things," and without the J & J consulting fees he wouldn't be able to buy her those "nice things." At least he was honest about his "nice things" status quo and ends justify the means integrity.

Regardless of whether you're trying to change a personal or professional status quo, you must identify and understand the motivations of anyone benefitting from the preservation of the existing status quo (your likely enemies) and who will benefit most from the new "reality" you're trying to create. Once you have an understanding of who your enemies might be and who your supporters should be, you can create a strategy to convert your lukewarm supporters into ardent supporters and neutralize your potential enemies as much as possible. Another lesson that I learned the hard way when my career, reputation, and net worth were destroyed by the keepers of various status quos is that you should delegate the status-quo-changing tasks as much as possible to depersonalize the attacks and spread the damage done by the keepers of the status quo you're trying to change. In other words, recruit supporters to create a change army instead of an army of one.

Think about the last personal or professional status quo you tried to change. Who were your "enemies" who wanted the old status quo to remain? Who were your supporters that would benefit from the new reality you were trying to create? What could you have done differently with your enemies and supporters to be more successful? And what would have been different for you?

I'll finish this chapter by once again suggesting that you apply the knowledge I just shared with you and make fully informed plans for changing your status quos:

- Make a list of two changes you want to make in your personal life in the next year. Write down what you stand to gain if you're successful and lose if you're unsuccessful. Make a list of those people who will support your proposed change and those who will be opposed to your change and what each of those people stand to gain and lose. Given all that you now know about your planned changes in your personal status quos, create a written plan to maximize the probability of your success. Include how you're going to recruit the most influential supporters and neutralize your most powerful opponents.
- Make a similar list and do the same for two changes you want to make in your professional life and career in the next year.

The legitimacy of most status quos seems to flow from "this is the way it has always been" and "this is the way it has always been done." As a result, every status quo at some point needs to be changed. As I learned the hard way, if a status quo is worth changing, it's worth careful planning to maximize your probability of success, and minimize the possibility that you will be destroyed in the process.

CHAPTER 9

THE PICKING YOUR BATTLES DILEMMA

Pick and wage your battles wisely, especially when it comes to the powers that be.

ACCORDING TO THE *Free Dictionary*, the idiom "pick your battles" means choosing "not to participate in minor, unimportant, or overly difficult arguments, contests, or confrontations, saving one's strength instead for those that will be of greater importance or where one has a greater chance of success." The only thing I would add to that definition is to pick only those battles in which the upside, namely what you have to gain, significantly outweighs the downside, namely what you have to lose.

According to that same *Free Dictionary*, the idiom "powers that be" means "the people or forces who are in a position of authority or control." The only thing I would add to that definition is that the powers that be are those with the power to positively or negatively impact your life, which is a broader definition than just those in authority or control.

With those definitions in mind, let's explore how well you've done at identifying the powers that be in your life and whether you've carefully picked and waged your battles with them. As part of your exploration, keep in mind that the powers that be often not only have the power to create the rules applied in your battle, but they can change those rules mid-battle to your detriment. Especially if the battle involves federal, state, or local elected officials or government employees. Also, when considering what you could have done differently in your past battles with the powers that be, ask yourself if the upside always outweighed the downside and whether you waged your battles behind closed doors. Lastly, ask yourself if you stayed focused on your goal or were you distracted by tangential battles that had little to do with your goal. In your battles, did you get angry, make it personal, publicly criticize, or question the powers that be?

1. Write down your natural reaction to disagreements, confrontations, and challenges from your origin programming. My origin programming taught me that whenever something very important to me was under attack, I should take everything personally, rely on me, myself and I, make that particular disagreement or battle and showing those particular bastards my highest priority, and immediately fight back with everything I had. Regardless of how significant the disagreement or threat. Regardless of how powerful the opponent. And regardless of how relevant that particular battle was to my personal and professional goals. Fire, ready, aim. Perfect.

2. Make a list of three "powers that be," namely people or groups that have negatively or positively impacted your personal life. The more powerful the better. It could be your significant other/spouse, the IRS, credit rating agencies,

health insurance companies, parents, an HOA, your bank/mortgage company, neighbors.

3. For each of those powers that be in your personal life, list two battles that you recently waged with them, one with a positive outcome and one with a negative outcome. Considering the definition of "pick your battles" and the outcomes of those battles, did you pick and wage each battle carefully? Did what you had to gain outweigh what you stood to lose? What would you have done differently to improve the outcome of the battles you won or lost? Would you have picked different battles or waged the battles you picked differently?

4. Make a list of three powers that be that have negatively or positively impacted your professional life. Once again, the more powerful the better. Professional life powers that be can include your boss, peers, subordinates, regulatory agencies, investors, customers and suppliers.

5. For each of those powers that be in your professional life, list two battles that you recently waged with them, one with a positive outcome and one with a negative outcome. Did you pick and wage each battle carefully? Did what you stood to gain outweigh what you could lose? What would you have done differently to improve the outcome of the battles you won or lost? Would you have picked different battles or waged the battles differently?

I earned a **PhD at Cyberonics** in how to ineffectively pick and wage battles with the powers that be. If I knew then what I know now, I'm certain I would have picked and waged the battles with the FDA, Senate Finance Committee, Wall Street, insurance companies, Medicare, the SEC, the *New York Times*, and various other large media outlets totally differently. And I probably would not have become the personal enemy of the many powerful powers that be who not only tragically destroyed the only FDA-approved treatment for people like my mother, but also destroyed my career, reputation, and net worth.

I paid dearly for the lessons that I'm about to share with you. If you are amazed that things like what I'm about to tell you can happen in the United States of America, so was I before they happened. And today they're happening more frequently than ever, in full public view. Every day we hear or read about another person who was destroyed personally, professionally, and/or financially without ever being charged or tried for an alleged crime because they dared disagree with, criticize, or challenge one of the powers that be. Every time you hear or read one of those stories, remember the lessons that I'm now sharing with you.

Cyberonics' device, the vagus nerve stimulator (VNS), had to meet incredibly stringent requirements for FDA approval. The FDA's rules and requirements for devices are different than those for drugs. VNS was the first device ever developed, studied, and submitted to the FDA for approval as a treatment for epilepsy. The FDA's device evaluation group had never reviewed any device for the treatment of epilepsy, so they brought in their drug counterparts who forced Cyberonics to do a second study as if its device was a drug, contrary to device regulations. Although the FDA's demand nearly bankrupted the company, Cyberonics did the second study and received FDA approval in 1997, four years later than it would have, had device regulations been properly applied.

As previously mentioned, powers that be often have the power to change the rules whenever they choose.

We thought the FDA approval process in depression would be considerably more straightforward, considering that the FDA, doctors, and patients had over ten years and 85,000 patient years' of positive experience with Cyberonics and our device. We also thought that the FDA would appoint a lead reviewer for our depression submission who knew our device. Wrong and wrong. The FDA appointed a lead reviewer who was new to the Neurological Devices Group and not only knew nothing about our device, but also had never been the lead reviewer for any device submission similar to ours. Just like his epilepsy colleagues who knew nothing about our device ten years earlier—when there were no device-based treatments for epilepsy—our inexperienced depression reviewer turned to his colleagues at the FDA's powerful antidepressant drug group for help. Predictably, the FDA's antidepressant drug group didn't like us, our device, or our studies that exceeded all device standards but didn't meet drug requirements. And in the case of treatment-resistant depression, showed that the already approved antidepressant drugs didn't work. Once again, just like with epilepsy, the FDA's antidepressant drug group convinced the device group that drug, not device, regulations should be applied to our device.

Drugs and devices like VNS are reviewed by advisory panels consisting of outside experts appointed by the FDA who make nonbinding recommendations that the FDA either approve or not approve the device or drug. In most cases, the FDA follows the panel's recommendation. At 5 p.m. the day before our depression advisory panel meeting, it became readily apparent that the FDA powers that be wanted the panel to recommend against approval when FDA informed us that a majority of the voting members for our panel were specially appointed from the FDA's antidepressant drug panel. This late notice was totally contrary to precedent and protocol. As was the special appointment of panel members with no device experience as the voting majority of a device panel. The deck was clearly stacked against us. Our device panel's recommendation would be controlled by voting members familiar only with drugs, drug standards, drug regulations, and drug definitions of valid scientific evidence in a nonresistant patient population instead of being familiar with device regulations and severe treatment-resistant depression.

The panel meeting was some eight hours long and unusually contentious. The FDA and their specially appointed panel couldn't have been more opposed to approval. Not because we didn't more than satisfy all device requirements for approval for use in a treatment-resistant population, but because we didn't satisfy drug requirements in a nonresistant patient population. Much to the FDA's dismay, we ultimately received a favorable five-to-two panel recommendation after we read the relevant device regulations and definitions of valid scientific evidence in our summation and exposed the fact the panel had never been properly trained by the FDA, and the Panel was refusing to properly apply device regulations to our device. If ever you've been called for jury duty and gotten to the *voir dire* phase of jury selection, you know that nothing will eliminate you from jury duty faster than if you refuse to apply the relevant laws. Obviously not the case with our advisory panel. Once again, the FDA powers that be had the power to change the rules. And did.

Although the FDA clearly wasn't pleased by the panel's recommendation, given that they'd previously approved every expedited-review device with a favorable panel recommendation like ours, we thought that approval in depression would be as straightforward as epilepsy approval which occured only nineteen days after the favorable Panel vote.

In the two months after the panel, two puzzling things occurred. First, contrary to precedent and protocol, the FDA wasn't talking to us like they did immediately after the epilepsy panel recommendation to jointly finalize the necessary documentation for approval. And secondly, although our stock almost doubled from $19 to $38 per share the day after the favorable panel recommendation, it steadily dropped to the mid-twenties over the next six weeks. What did the FDA and Wall Street powers that be know that we didn't?

Without the dignity of any dialogue, sixty days after the favorable panel recommendation we had our answer when, out of the blue, the FDA faxed us a not-approvable letter during a quarterly earnings conference call with Wall Street and our public shareholders. Interesting timing, wouldn't you say? In that letter, the FDA reiterated everything they said at the panel to justify their not-approvable position, including that we needed to do another three-year study that psychiatric opinion leaders said was neither feasible, ethical, nor safe, and would cost Cyberonics over $30 million. It was as if the FDA completely disregarded the seven years and $50 million spent on studies; our extraordinary, highly significant one-year data in the most depressed patient population ever studied; the unique sustained and accumulating long-term safety and efficacy of VNS; the opinions of over a hundred psychiatric thought leaders; the opinions of hundreds of patients and the leading depression patient advocacy groups; and the vote of the FDA's own handpicked panel of experts. They were adamant that antidepressant drug regulations should be applied to our device. And they were the powers that be who made and changed the rules whenever it suited them.

Cyberonics and I as CEO had approximately twelve hours before the market opened the next day to write and issue a press release and hold a conference call with investors to break this very bad news and inform our investors how we planned to deal with it. Nobody at the FDA was available to talk. In epilepsy, Cyberonics acquiesced and did another expensive study that all but bankrupted the company. There was no reason to do the same with depression. Our case for approval was considerably stronger. However, there was no precedent for picking and waging such a battle. Has anyone ever overturned a not-approvable letter? Has anyone ever fought with the FDA and won? Did the FDA tip off Wall Street? What should we tell investors? I talked to everyone who I thought could help: The board of directors, including the former speaker of the US House of Representatives and chairman and CEO of one of the largest device companies in the world, our entire senior management team, the preeminent psychiatrists we were working most closely with and who had presented to the panel, legal counsel including FDA counsel in DC who had previously worked for the FDA for over twenty-five years. Although it may sound funny now, the consensus then was (1) this was a first for everyone, (2) the FDA clearly wanted another study contrary to device regulations, (3) we were in trouble, and (4) you need to go to Washington, Skip, and figure it out.

Of course the other consultant I had during those twelve hours was myself . . . the Skip Cummins shaped and steeled by my origin programming to never walk away from any fight, rely primarily on "me, myself, and I," and "show the bastards." What I desperately needed and didn't have was the knowledge I have now or a confidante with the knowledge I have now. As a result, the decisions I made and my actions as Cyberonics' CEO following receipt of the FDA's not-approvable letter arguably "won the battle" by generating FDA approval of our device for treatment-resistant depression but it also caused us to lose the war. Meaning that my reliance on my unrevised origin programming ultimately cost more than four million Americans with treatment-resistant depression access to the only FDA-approved treatment for their very specific life-threatening illness and cost me my career, reputation, and net worth. That is one very big accountability pill to swallow and one I needed to swallow to master me and help you master you from the inside out.

My personal and Cyberonics' battle with the FDA began the day after we received the not-approvable letter when Cyberonics issued a press release that was followed by an investor conference call hosted by me and a live TV interview with CNBC. Contrary to what I now know about picking and waging battles carefully, especially with powers that be, Cyberonics and I immediately made several fatal mistakes:

1. **We criticized the FDA:** Cyberonics—and I as its CEO—criticized the FDA for being uninformed and ignoring regulations, the unmet needs of millions of Americans, and experts' opinions, including the vote of their handpicked advisory panel.

2. **We declared war prematurely** before we had a plan and a strategy, thereby limiting our options for "peace."

3. **We called out the FDA publicly:** We shared with the public our criticism of and our intention to fight with the FDA.

4. **I made it personal:** It was abundantly clear from the press release, conference call, and CNBC interview that I was angry at our FDA lead reviewer and others at the FDA who made their unjustifiable not-approvable decision.

5.

Had I known then what I know about from whence I came and about carefully choosing my battles with the powers that be, the tone and wording of the press release, Wall Street conference call, and CNBC interview would have been much different. Cyberonics and I would have avoided all the mistakes listed above by simply stating: (1) More than four million Americans with treatment-resistant depression have no FDA-approved treatment option, (2) ours was the first device of its kind deemed not-approvable by the FDA, (3) we were disappointed and saddened by the decision, and (4) we planned to work diligently with the FDA to understand the basis for the decision and submit the additional information and data required for approval. In other words, the plan we communicated should have been one of cooperation with FDA not fighting consisent with my origin programming.

Over the next four months, with the advice of our lobbyist and outside regulatory counsel who'd worked at the FDA for twenty years, I met with everyone in Washington, DC, who would meet with me to understand what happened and help Cyberonics get a fair hearing at the FDA.

Our outside regulatory counsel, who was well known and highly respected at the FDA, and I met first with our lead reviewer, his boss and his boss's boss. These were the three people primarily responsible for the not-approvable decision and were now, thanks in part to the mistakes we made with the press release, conference call, and CNBC interview, predictably hostile toward me and VNS. Much to our amazement, FDA informed us that their not-approvable decision was based on the Panel's deliberations, not the Panel's vote. FDA also told us that they didn't have time to properly train the specially deputized drug panel members on device regulations and definition of valid scientific evidence. Which by the way is totally contrary to regulation. In other words, FDA told us that their not approvable decision was the direct result of their failure to follow regulations. What?!? Yessir, Mr. Cummins, we're the FDA powers that be and you're not. And we make and change the rules whenever it suits us. Or said another way, our not approvable ends in your case justify whatever means we needed to get there including ignoring regulations and the Panel's vote.

Their message was loud and clear: *We made our decision and there's no way given what you said in your press release, on your conference call, or during your CNBC interview that you're getting approval without another study.* It was obvious this was now a very personal, very public fight between the three of them and me. Clearly the press release, conference call and CNBC interview made things a lot worse and weren't in the best interests of 4.4 million Americans with treatment-resistant depression, Cyberonics, or its stakeholders. If I only knew then what I know now or had a confidante who did.

Our outside counsel, our lobbyist, and I agreed that we needed to rally support among the powers that be in Washington to have any hope of prevailing. We next met with the device ombudsman—the head of the FDA's device complaint department—and his boss, the most senior device person at the FDA. Our outside regulatory counsel had long-standing relationships with both. Suddenly, more powerful FDA powers that be were paying attention to our "data," including a summary of FDA's highly unusual review and not-approvable decision process, a comparison of our studies and device regulations, and a summary of the safety and effectiveness of our device in patients who had been treated for depression for an average of eighteen years and had failed to respond to an average of eighteen treatments, including drugs, drug combinations, and electroshock therapy.

Our lobbyist and I also met with as many senators and members of congress as possible and asked them for their help in determining why the FDA ignored their handpicked panel of experts, and what we needed to do to convince regulators to give us a fair hearing. I later learned the FDA was contacted by more senators and members of congress on our behalf than ever before, including powerful Democratic Senator Ted Kennedy, Republican Speaker of the House Tom DeLay, and Libertarian senator, Dr. Ron Paul. The message to the FDA was that Congress was watching and expected the FDA to follow all applicable regulations in our case. Simultaneously, FDA's head of devices was receiving hundreds of letters supporting approval from experts in psychiatry, psychiatrists, patients, patient advocacy groups, and others.

In my conversations with FDA's head of devices, senators, and members of congress, I let them know that we would soon have two-year data that was even more compelling than the one-year data that was the basis for the panel's recommendation and the FDA's not-approvable decision. We would soon give the FDA the face-saving "out" they needed to follow device regulations and the panel's recommendation and approve our device based on a new submission with new, more compelling safety and effectiveness data.

In order to seriously consider our new data, FDA's head of devices needed the blessing of even more powerful FDA powers that be. This resulted in our lobbyist and me being invited to a three-hour meeting in the FDA Commissioner's Office. A number of important people from FDA attended, including the agency's deputy commissioner and chief medical officer, who was previously the head of the drug side of the FDA when most of the antidepressants were approved, and the FDA's deputy commissioner for policy, who had fielded all the calls and responded to all the letters from elected officials. Also attending was the general counsel for US Department of Health and Human Services—the highest-ranking lawyer overseeing the FDA. Our fight had obviously gotten the attention of the most powerful powers that be at the FDA and in Washington. Neither FDA's head of devices nor any FDA officials who issued the not-approvable decision attended. The purpose of the meeting was for me to present all of our data, including our new two-year data, to the FDA's chief medical officer and for her to give her thumbs-up or thumbs-down to reconsider the not-approvable decision.

The meeting seemed to go well. The chief medical officer gave FDA's head of devices the thumbs-up for reconsideration and we immediately submitted our new, even more compelling two-year data. Our lobbyist was amazed that without any formal medical training, I not only held my own, but actually impressed the FDA's chief medical officer with my knowledge. I was flattered by the compliments but, as I told her, "It's my job."

One unsettling moment, which turned out to be a bad omen, occurred before the meeting. The first person to leave a separate meeting that occurred before ours in the same conference room was none other than our lead reviewer and leader of the not-approvable gang. He looked at me straight in the eye and smirked. I soon found out why: he was about to show me who was boss in this highly personal battle for professional survival that I had mistakenly created. Never underestimate the power of any of the powers that be in your life, including government bureaucrats. Especially government bureaucrats. And especially lower level ones.

The next card played by the FDA not approvable powers that be resulted in a forty-page warning letter from the agency's regional compliance office in Dallas stating, among other things, that our manufacturing processes were out of control, we were underreporting serious adverse events, and that our product was unsafe. Had the warning letter been accurate, we never would have received FDA approval for depression and would have been at serious risk of the FDA shutting us down. Instead, after I met with the regional office's senior management and pointed out the warning letter's numerous inaccuracies, and we submitted a six-volume response, the warning letter was officially closed in record time, paving the way for an approvable letter telling us that. subject to only a few straightforward conditions, VNS would be approved as a treatment for severe treatment-resistant depression.

That approvable letter came in February 2005, only seven months after we received the initial not-approvable letter. An unprecedented turnaround in record time! Our board of directors, psychiatrists, Wall Street, the media, and people who hoped to use our device were stunned and amazed by what we had accomplished. Our stock price and total market value jumped from a low of $13 per share and $312 million following the not-approvable letter to a record high of $45 a share and $1.1 billion. Most everyone was elated. Some were not. The media and Wall Street analysts who were proven wrong, and short sellers who lost millions of dollars betting that we would never get approval were especially incensed. They were angry with me for not sharing the positive progress we were making behind closed doors with the FDA prior to receiving the approvable letter that I knew was coming. Once again, my list of powers that be who considered me the enemy was growing quickly.

We thought the approvable letter was evidence we had won the battle. We thought we were now on the cusp of commercializing the only FDA-approved treatment for severe treatment-resistant depression that could give millions of people like my mother hope.

Little did we know.

We've all heard about the wrath of a woman scorned. My experience says that there is no wrath like that of a government bureaucrat scorned. Especially a government bureaucrat who can summon one of the most powerful powers that be in the United States Senate.

At the time of our approvable letter, unknown to us, thanks to public investigations of a number of FDA-approved drugs starting with Vioxx, the chairman of the Senate Finance Committee (SFC), which has control of Medicare and Medicaid funding, had become the go-to person for every FDA whistleblower with an ax to grind and/or an ego and career to save. According to the Senate Finance Committee report, our lead reviewer called the SFC chairman's office shortly after we received the approvable letter, *falsely alleging* that (1) VNS was neither safe nor effective for depression, (2) every FDA scientist who reviewed our data was against approval, and (3) the FDA's approval decision was politically motivated by congressional pressure created by my illegal campaign contributions, including a $100,000 contribution to the Republican National Committee! Clearly the FDA powers that be were calling in the most powerful powers that be in the U.S. Senate to prove they were right and destroy VNS for treatment resistant depression and me.

Now is as good a time as any for me to contrast what the FDA not-approvable gang and others did throughout this entire process to destroy Cyberonics and me, with what Cyberonics did which was to always play by the rules and comply with all laws and regulations. Perhaps all the false allegations thrown at Cyberonics and me were simply projections of the accusers' own values. One of the many lessons I learned the hard way in my dealings with the FDA, Wall Street, and other powers that be is that one should be very careful about projecting your values onto the powers that be, especially when those powers have shown that their values are completely different than yours.

We had no idea the FDA not-approvable crowd had gone "nuclear" until May of 2005, when we were blindsided by a Senate Finance Committee letter demanding our cooperation in its investigation of the FDA's approvable decision. The letter began by reminding us not so subtly that SFC controlled Medicare and Medicaid funding and, by implication, reimbursement of all drugs and devices, including ours.

We pledged our total cooperation and, based on the advice of outside counsel who said the SFC "investigation" would have no bearing whatsoever on FDA approval, we didn't publicly disclose the letter. Apparently SFC wasn't happy with our decision. Two weeks later, I received a call from a *Wall Street Journal* reporter who wanted my comment on the committee's investigation of Cyberonics regarding the FDA approvable decision. I checked with our legal counsel and learned indirectly from a *Wall Street Journal* editor that the SFC had leaked the letter to the *Journal*. We now had no choice. I called the reporter back and set the record straight. Neither Cyberonics nor I were being investigated, the FDA was, and we were cooperating fully. The next day, when the article ran, we issued a short press release before the market opened. It simply stated that we had received a letter requesting certain documents and were fully cooperating. But we also held a conference call.

At this point if you're thinking, "Oh, no. Not again," you're doing so for good reason. When investors on the call accused Cyberonics of withholding material information because we didn't immediately disclose the letter on the day we received it, I felt an obligation to provide all the relevant facts. To defend my and the company's integrity. I explained that outside counsel advised us that disclosure wasn't necessary because neither the letter nor the Senate Finance Committee's investigation of the FDA's decision would have any impact on ultimate FDA approval.

Unfortunately I didn't stop there. I then explained we were forced to issue a press release by the Senate Finance Committee allegedly leaking the letter to the *Wall Street Journal*. There was absolutely no need for me to have mentioned that. I should have simply said we disclosed the letter when we did simply because the *Wall Street Journal* called us with inaccurate information that needed to be corrected. Before implicitly or explicitly criticizing one of the most powerful committees in the U.S. Senate, and one of the most powerful powers that be with the most significant impact on Cyberonics and VNS, I should have measured what Cyberonics had to gain or lose and realized that it was all "lose," because, best case, SFC might be neutral regarding VNS. Worst case, SFC could become my and patients' worst nightmare, which is exactly what happened.

We should have cooperated with the committee's requests but otherwise refrained from any comment. If I only knew then what I know now or had a confidante who did.

In July 2005, despite our FDA review team's best efforts and the SFC's letter and investigation, we received final FDA approval for treatment-resistant depression. In August, VNS surpassed 100,000 total patient years of experience. We were consistently beating Wall Street analysts' expectations, and our stock remained near a record high. We were on a roll. Or so we thought.

In November 2005, I received a call one evening I'll never forget. Specifically from an agent with the FBI's Government Threats Task Force, informing me that I had been named a person of interest in the assault and attempted murder of the SFC chairman's chief investigator. A week later I was interviewed in my office not only by the FBI agent but also an Arlington, Virginia, homicide detective for roughly four hours. My then-wife, who grew up in the Soviet Union, warned me that I had obviously made enemies in the government and that if I were in the Soviet

Union, I would have already "disappeared." She encouraged me to resign from Cyberonics immediately, sell my stock, and voluntarily "disappear." I told her not to worry—that things were different in America and that the truth, facts, and data would prevail. My decision to ignore her advice and stay at Cyberonics and continue the fight consistent with my origin programming proved to be more costly than I could ever imagine.

The SFC was far from done with me and Cyberonics. In February 2006, it took the largely unprecedented step of releasing an almost four hundred page report on the FDA's improper approval of VNS for treatment-resistant depression on the floor of the US Senate. The report, in essence, said that VNS for TRD was neither safe nor effective, that the FDA should never have approved it, and that Medicare and Medicaid shouldn't pay for it. Predictably, the staff that prepared the report never interviewed any psychiatrists familiar with TRD or involved in our studies, any patients suffering from TRD, any patients treated with VNS, any patient-advocacy organizations, or any mechanism-of-action experts regarding how and why VNS works in depression..

Still completely ignorant of the knowledge I'm now sharing with you—and counterproductive to Cyberonics' mission—we issued another press release with more of the same irrational battle picking and waging, and public criticism and disagreement. *What* was I thinking? The answer is I wasn't thinking. I was simply following my origin programming and repeating the same mistakes I previously made at Cyberonics, which were dooming VNS for TRD, my commitment to my mother, and my career, reputation, and net worth. VNS for TRD may have been FDA approved, but it would never be covered or reimbursed by Medicare, Medicaid, or any major insurance company and, as a result, would never be available to over 4.4 million Americans suffering from TRD. If I only knew then what I know now and am sharing in this book!

By May of 2006, more than twenty articles had been published in leading peer-reviewed journals and the long-term data from our studies continued to be the star at meetings of groups like the annual American Psychiatric Association. More than 2,600 psychiatrists had prescribed VNS to over 10,000 patients. Yet only 1,100 patients with severe treatment resistant depression had started treatment. Why? Because insurance companies—the powers that be in terms of what drugs and devices are used to treat which patients in the United States—can deny coverage for any device or drug they deem "experimental" or "investigational," even those with FDA approval. Without any medical malpractice liability whatsoever. Even though MDs employed by the insurance companies are making treatment decisions. Which is exactly what every major payer was doing with VNS, thanks in large part to the Senate Finance Committee report.

Making enemies of the FDA not-approvable powers that be and their powerful SEC allies proved to be a very costly mistake. The SFC report and comments by FDA personnel and various SFC senators' staff members were cited in refusals by many major insurance companies, like Blue Cross/Blue Shield and Medicare, to extend their favorable VNS coverage for epilepsy to VNS for depression. In addition, these same powers that be no doubt played a significant role in my demise. When the Securities and Exchange Commission began its inquiry of Cyberonics' stock options in June 2006. FDA personnel and SFC staffers in all likelihood effectively "encouraged" the SEC to give me no benefit of the doubt. VNS for depression and I didn't stand a chance versus three of the most powerful powers that be in the federal government namely FDA, SFC and the SEC.

Not all my interactions as CEO of Cyberonics with the powers that be were adversarial. After we received the not-approvable letter, I met with many senators and members of congress to ask for their help. Apparently I was successful because a record number of them called or wrote letters to the FDA asking for an explanation and/or assurances that our new submission would be reviewed consistent with regulations and the best interests of millions of Americans with severe depression. Needless to say Cyberonics and I were very grateful for their support.

Cyberonics and my interactions with FDA senior management were also obviously successful since we ultimately received FDA approval despite the numerous roadblocks created by the FDA not-approvable bunch.

So why do you think I was successful with these powers that be? There are several possible reasons. We in no way threatened them or their status quo. We never criticized or disagreed with them. We kept all of our discussions behind closed doors and out of the public eye. Because many of the senators and members of congress who contacted the FDA no doubt had family members with severe depression, who might have benefited from an FDA-approved treatment, our interests were likely aligned. We didn't ask them to stick their necks out and tell the FDA to approve our device. We simply asked them for their help in convincing the FDA to do the right thing and review our new two-year data consistent with regulations and the needs of millions of Americans. Lastly, the senators and member of congress who contacted the FDA didn't seem interested in the allegations of relatively junior FDA whistleblowers. They had confidence that senior FDA management would sort out fact from fiction, consistent with regulations.

As for FDA senior management, unlike the FDA not-approvable bunch, they were totally committed to strictly following device regulations and going by the book, especially given the Congressional oversight involved in our specific case. Needless to say, FDA senior management didn't take it easy on us, our two-year data, or psychiatrists and mechanism-of-action experts supporting approval. If anything, senior management's review of our data was more rigorous than the review by the not-approvable bunch. And the post-approval studies demanded by FDA senior management went beyond what was recommended by the panel. Too bad the not-approvable bunch didn't defer to those with considerably more seniority and authority and knowledge of the regulations and data in the first place. And too bad I didn't know then what I know now which is never underestimate the power of any of the powers that be in your life, and pick your battles with the powers that be *very* carefully.

I have many more "pick your battles" very carefully—especially with the "powers that be"—experiences to share with you from both my professional and personal lives, but will hold those for the next time our paths cross. Although I've limited the experiences I've shared with you here to powers that be in my professional life, the pick-your-battles challenge in our personal lives is every bit as important. Broadly define the powers that be in your personal life to include all those that can positively or negatively impact your life—including your spouse/significant other, your kids, friends, neighbors, the DMV, the IRS, credit rating agencies, health insurance companies, parents, homeowners associations, your bank/mortgage lenders—so that you pick your battles very carefully.

Here are a few lessons from my sixty years of experience to help you pick and wage your battles wisely:

1. Know from whence you came so that you can predict your natural reaction to any disagreement.

2. Broadly define the powers that be in your professional and personal lives as those that can have a positive or negative impact on your life.

3. Pick and wage your battles very carefully and avoid battles where the downside exceeds the upside.

4. Never make public any battle with any powers that be; keep all disagreements behind closed doors.

5. Avoid appearing as though you are fighting the powers that be.

6. Always appear to be agreeing and cooperating with, not arguing with or criticizing, the powers that be.

7. Try to align the interests of the powers that be with yours.

8. Never provoke the powers that be who appear to be your adversaries.

9. Do everything in your power to keep from becoming a personal enemy of any of the powers that be.

10. Depersonalize any disagreement or battle with all powers that be by delegating/deferring to as many others as possible and recruiting as many supporters as possible.

11. Stay focused on YOUR goal; don't engage in any unnecessary fights with the powers that be.

CHAPTER 10

HOW TO WIN WHEN "SHIT" HAPPENS

According to *Wikipedia*, "shit happens" is a slang phrase that is used as a simple existential observation that life is full of unpredictable events. The more polite French equivalent being *c'est la vie*, meaning "That's life."

MANY PHILOSOPHERS AND gurus have commented on "shit" happening being part of life, including Forrest Gump:

Man to Forrest Gump, "Whoa, man, you just ran through a big pile of dog shit!"

Forrest Gump, "It happens."

Man, "What, shit?"

Forrest Gump, "Sometimes."

If bad things and "shit" are simply part of life, the more important dilemma is how we deal with those bad things and still win. In Forrest Gump's case, he admitted that shit happening was part of life and he kept running. His view seems to differ from the *Wikipedia* definition in that, according to Forrest, "shit" happening includes both predictable and unpredictable events. Most businesses and sports teams seem to agree with Forrest Gump in that they plan for the predictable and have a process for dealing with the unpredictable. In sports, predictable and unpredictable bad things include fouls, penalties, turnovers, errors, injuries, ejections, suspensions, and trades. Many sports teams win because they expect, anticipate, and do everything in their power to minimize and deal with all bad things, even completely unexpected and unanticipated bad things.

In order for us to win in life don't we need plans and a process to deal with all the inevitable, sometimes predictable, sometimes unpredictable "shit" that happens? My answer is an emphatic *yes* based on my experience. Let's see how you feel at the end of this chapter once we've explored how you and I have handled some of the bad things that are part of life. In this chapter, instead of asking you all the questions upfront, let's change the order a bit by considering one bad thing at a time.

One of the most common bad things we all face in life is the end of a marriage, a committed relationship, or a significant romantic relationship. Especially one that involves cohabitation and/or children. I have had two long marriages end in divorce. How about you? Think about one relationship that ended.

- How long did the relationship last?
- Were you cohabitating?
- Were children involved? If so, what ages? Were they your children with a previous spouse/partner, your partner's or both of yours?
- What caused the end of the relationship?
- When did the problems that ended the relationship first appear?
- What did you do to try to fix those problems?
- Why didn't those potential fixes work?
- What specifically did you, your partner, or both of you do that caused the relationship to end?

- What could you and your partner have done to anticipate the problems that ended your relationship and implement fixes before they became problems?
- How did you react to the relationship ending? What did you do to heal yourself, children, friends, etc.?
- What did you learn from your experience and what will/did you do differently in your next relationship to ensure that history doesn't repeat itself?

If "shit happens" in life refers only to unpredictable events, then it cannot, in most cases, be used to explain the end of a relationship. Why? Because there are hundreds if not thousands of books and articles that provide us with the most common causes for breakups. That list includes money problems, addictions, shifting priorities, loss of intimacy or connection, disinterest in sex, and cheating. If we know the primary causes of break-ups and divorce and one or more of those causes caused my or your divorce, then our divorce was predictable, not unpredictable. And being predictable, by definition, it may have been preventable if the known causes were discussed with our spouse/partner early and often.

Having been married twice for eighteen and twenty-one years, respectively, and having raised two children in my twenty-one-year marriage, I've seen a lot of marital good, bad, and ugly and have contributed my fair share to all three. In neither marriage did we anticipate, expect, or have a plan to minimize the common causes of divorce. In other words, we never discussed the predictable issues that eventually cause major problems in many marriages, our differences, and how those differences might cause problems in the future. We also didn't create a process to resolve issues before they arose or immediately after. We also never discussed our goals. If I knew then what I know now, and had created plans and a process to deal with the predictable and unpredictable events that emotionally, spiritually, sexually, or legally end marriages, I'd still likely be happily married.

One of the things I discovered about being married is that life often gets in the way of the love, commitment, and devotion that brings people together in the first place. Other things become higher priorities than the connection, intimacy, and oneness that were integral parts of the relationship in the early years. Having been on both the giving and receiving end of spousal/ significant-other deprioritization, I know from experience how devastating it is to go from being the highest priority to suddenly being a low priority whose feelings don't matter. Especially when those feelings are discounted with a literal or figurative, "If your life's so miserable why don't you do something about it?" or "Don't be ridiculous, I still love you" Or "Stop projecting." The former is what my first wife repeatedly said to me when she totally deprioritized me and our marriage in favor of her law career. The second I unfortunately said to my second wife and mother of my children when my career and our children became all-consuming and caused me to deprioritize our marriage and her. And the third my former Southern California significant other repeatedly said to me whenever my hurt feelings were inconsistent with her reality.

Here's my answer to the question I asked you about what you could have done to anticipate the problems and implement fixes before your relationship ended. Knowing what I know now, I would have given my second marriage and relationship with my wife at least the same priority as my career so that she didn't feel deprioritized. I would have done a much better job of communicating with my wife by together anticipating and planning to resolve predictable problems and compassionately listening to and acting on her feelings. Specifically, here is what I would have done differently to maintain the extraordinary intimacy, mutual trust and respect, reciprocity, love, devotion, and commitment that characterized our relationship in the early years:

1. **Created a process to deal with the unpredictable.** Regarding unpredictable events, I would have developed a process for my wife and I to immediately deal with them. For instance, we could have agreed on safe times and places to share our feelings with one another and together find a solution.

2. **Developed plans to deal with the predictable.** Regarding the predictable things that end relationships, I would have discussed those with my wife either before we were married or in our first years of marriage and developed a plan for how we were going to prevent and deal with them when and if they appeared. I had eighteen years of prior experience and knew what typically caused marriages to end, but I didn't do anything with that knowledge and experience in my second marriage. I wish I had.

3. **Respected and had compassion for my spouse's feelings and paid attention to clear warning signs.** Compassion is defined as "sympathetic consciousness of others distress together with a desire to alleviate it." Instead of discounting my wife's feelings when my wife told me she felt she had been deprioritized in favor of my career and children, that I wasn't looking at her or

paying as much attention to her as I used
to, that we didn't have the extraordinary
intimacy or oneness we once had and I didn't
seem to be very interested in sex or her as a
woman, I should have been compassionate
by listening, asking her for examples, and
asking her what I could do differently. Then
I should have immediately come up with a
written plan she agreed with to address her
very real feelings and the problems I was
unintentionally creating in our marriage.
The same way she saw me handle problems
at Cyberonics with the management team,
the board, investors, and the FDA. Instead I
unintentionally discounted her feelings by
trying to use logic (typical male response)
to explain to her why her feelings (emotions
being primarily feminine) were not
supported by facts and therefore illogical.

What I never understood until it was too late was that every
time I tried to explain away her feelings with logic, I only wors-
ened the situation from her perspective by reiterating that her
feelings didn't matter and she and our marriage weren't a high
priority for me. Of course, the more I implicitly discounted her
feelings, the less interested she was in sharing her feelings and the
more hurt and angry she became. The more hurt and angry she
became, the more I thought she didn't appreciate all the sacrifices
I was making for her and our family by working ninety-plus-hour
weeks and creating extraordinary abundance (except, of course,
the emotional abundance she needed). I didn't understand her
emotions. She didn't understand my logic. She eventually felt

taken for granted and ignored. And I eventually felt taken for granted and devalued.

Predictably we ultimately sought the validation we originally received from each other and our marriage from other people, places, and things, including divorce. Was Dr. Spock on *Star Trek* married? I don't think so, but if he were married to a human woman, it probably didn't last long, since masculine logic and feminine emotions fall into the "never the twain shall meet" category.

SEX! Now that I have your attention, let's talk about another reason many relationships end. Based on what I experienced in my marriages, what I've observed in other couples I know well, and what I learned during my five years of tantra training and teaching: unfulfilling, boring, unsatisfying sex often becomes *the* major issue for many couples. So why is sex such a major problem and relationship killer? According to the construction workers with whom I shoveled concrete for many summers when I was in college, it's all about the beans in the jar. Whenever the subject of marriage came up, they told me don't do it, because "if you put a bean in a jar for every time you make love (they used a different word/phrase) to your wife the year before you're married and take a bean out of the jar every time you make love after you're married, you'll die with a lot of beans in the jar." Believe it or not, my experience in two long marriages and five years of tantra training, teaching, and practice as a certified tantra educator suggests that if you interpret the construction workers' answer to the question as "there's not enough of it," meaning good *sex* in marriage, then the construction workers were more right than wrong. Too bad I can't show you photos of my construction worker sex therapists and marriage counselors; you would think I had completely lost my mind. Hang on. Let me explain.

Neuroscience, believe it or not, agrees with the construction workers' beans in the jar explanation. According to research, the neurochemicals of love and attachment, such as oxytocin, dissipate within the first four years of a relationship. So then what happens? Sex and lovemaking become boring. Men and women lose interest in being with each other. Marriages can become sexless. Many marriages become all about the kids. If alcohol or drugs are involved, relationships can become toxic.

Many men and women seek some sort of alchemy to replace the lost chemistry in their relationship. The traditional individual alchemy being affairs. Intellectual, emotional, energetic, and/or sexual affairs with other men and women, hobbies, alcohol or drugs, etc. that divert your time, energies, emotions, attention from your significant other and your marriage/relationship, and in many cases cause great pain, shame, and guilt to those involved. Before you start flirting, sharing energies, etc. with someone else, why not flirt with, share energies with, and have an affair with your spouse? Whatever you find exciting about an "affair," do the same with your spouse/significant other.

Other forms of alchemy that some couples resort to are swingers clubs, porn, and polyamory which means having another lover with the blessing of your partner. Why couples who feel like their relationship has been deprioritized or are already having problems with sex think it's a good idea to invite other "partners" into their relationship is beyond me. Foolishly been there, done that. Don't go there.

Tantra has been proven over a thousand years to be another of the many other forms of alchemy that couples can use to rediscover the "spark" in their relationships. Like everything, it doesn't work for everyone, but it worked for me and many others I observed during my five years of training and teaching.

Little did I know that Grandma Bowie was teaching me tantra when she told me, "You'll never love anyone else until you love yourself." Tantra is indeed based on that age-old principle that you realize your full potential in life, especially in relationships, when you first love yourself. Tantra teaches us how to love ourselves by teaching us from whence we came and how to use tantra techniques to get rid of all the negative energies, pain, shame, and guilt baggage we're carrying around from the past. Tantra then teaches us how to use the same techniques to summon and share all the magnificence, beauty, power, pleasure, and bliss within us when and with whom we choose.

Many people think tantra is all about sex. A lot people think that tantra and porn are close to the same thing. Not the tantra that I know, which is the antithesis to porn and teaches us how to experience pleasure and bliss, including orgasmic bliss, without traditional sex. Tantra or tantra yoga as it's often called, is ancient Tao and Hindu yoga, breathing and sounding, meditation and massage techniques combined with organic vagus nerve stimulation (yes, the very science Cyberonics pioneered and commercialized) to help us become awakened and empowered masters of our energies and energy bodies. Tantra teaches that sexual energies, as distinguished from physical sex, are life-force energies, meaning that our sexual energies create life, both literally as in offspring and figuratively as in happy, healthy relationships, personally and professionally, with ourselves and with others. Most importantly, tantra teaches us that we don't need traditional sex, with all its performance anxiety and personal boundary issues, to summon and share extraordinary pleasure and bliss, including orgasmic bliss, with ourselves and others.

Are you happier and more productive personally and professionally and is your marriage and relationship with your significant other stronger, more vibrant, more fulfilling when what you define as your "sex life" is good? If so, keeping reading or listening.

I embraced tantra in large part because I helped pioneer and completely understood vagus nerve stimulation, the science explaining how and why tantra works. The vagus nerve connects every one of the tantra energy centers in the body, called chakras, with the brain. As we proved at Cyberonics, the signals in the left vagus go upward from the body to the brain, informing and enlightening it. Vagus nerve stimulation using an implantable device or tantra techniques, such as breathing and sounding, massage, yoga, etc., favorably modulates the areas of the brain and neurotransmitters that control depression, anxiety, memory, reward, pleasure, fear, orgasm. Tantra is no longer some sort of Tao and Hindu voodoo. It's science.

Tantra is near the top of my list of things I know now that I wish I knew then. At least in time to save my twenty-one-year marriage. Tantra taught me and can teach you how to summon and share the most extraordinary positive energies, including love and sexual energies and even more important, without traditional sex. We are taught from a very early age that extraordinary pleasure and bliss, including orgasmic bliss, comes almost exclusively from having intercourse. Tantra teaches us that the same pleasure and bliss can be summoned and shared through unconditional giving and receiving using tantra techniques without even kissing! I'm not kidding. Before I opened my mind and tried tantra, I would have thought that what I just wrote was total BS. Not now!

One of the many things that beginners learn in a tantra weekend is how to solve the beans in the jar problem. The men and women are divided up with the men being taught how to honor, nurture, and worship their "goddess" the tantra way. Meaning no kissing, oral sex, or intercourse. Meaning no need for an erection! The class starts by the men being asked, "Do you often come home from work interested in lovemaking only to have your significant other tell you that she's tired, has a headache etc.?" When the men all nod knowingly, of course likely thinking it's the woman's problem, they are then asked, "Do you think her response would be different if every time you touched her she had an orgasm?" The male students laugh nervously because they understand that they are as much, if not more, the problem than their female partner.

The women are separately taught how to receive the honoring, nurturing, and worshipping they are about to receive from their male partners . . . without kissing, oral sex, intercourse, or their partner having an erection. Learning how to become a "masterful receiver," which sounds totally oxymoronic, is another of the very important skills that tantra can teach you. Why? Because once again, we are taught that we have to do something to *earn* the attention, pleasure, and bliss being given to us by our partner instead of just receiving their unconditional gift. Think about it: even when our partner is giving to us unconditionally, because we can't receive unconditionally, we discount the pleasure and bliss we're receiving—the beautiful gift—by thinking and worrying about what we need to give back. Talk about a senseless distraction. In tantra, we're taught that receivers are also givers because their unconditional receiving maximizes the pleasure and bliss they are experiencing and in turn sharing with the giver.

If you watch professional sports on TV, you're probably familiar with the commercials about the dreaded ED—erectile dysfunction. Meaning when the time is right, you or your "little man" is wrong. "C'mon dude, don't go dysfunctional on me again!" Talk about major injuries. You know it's a huge problem, or we think it's a huge problem, given all the money the drug companies spend on ads for their ED drugs. (By the way, I don't understand how a certain ED drug solves my problem if, after I take it, my wife and I sit in separate bathtubs holding hands watching the sunset. Does that mean if I have an erection she doesn't even get to see it, let alone touch it?) Anyway, we have been brainwashed into thinking that getting it up and keeping it up for an hour or two or three is every real, functional man's birthright, regardless of age. We've also been totally brainwashed into thinking that an erection is the only way for men to experience and share orgasmic bliss with a woman. If you continue to embrace this brainwashing, like I did for the first fifty-eight years of my life, you and your significant other will miss more beauty, love, pleasure, and bliss than you ever knew existed, in all aspects of your life. If I only knew then what I know now.

One of the lessons I learned after I moved to Southern California is that we can create self-fulfilling prophecies of predictable shit happening by not knowing or ignoring what we're good at, what we're looking for and the traits of the type of person we're compatible with in relationships. As regards dating and relationships, I was dazed and confused since I had only recently become a single empty nester for the first time in my adult life. A life coach helped me find some clarity by making lists of the ideal traits of women that I was most compatible with and available to date and types of relationships for which I was available. My list included a committed monogamous relationship but excluded cohabitation and marriage. The list of traits of an ideal female partner included empty nester with no children at home, at least one successful marriage or committed monogamous relationship of at least ten years, a history of honoring commitments and living with integrity, financial security meaning income that produced a satisfactory lifestyle, geographic flexibility to relocate, personal and professional commitments that permitted spontaneous travel, a civil relationship with previous spouses/significant others, good mental and physical health and an open minded tolerance of different spiritual, nutritional, political and religious beliefs. The good news is that I had my lists. The bad news is that I created a self-fulfilling prophecy of predictable shit happening when I largely ignored my lists and ended up in a two year relationship that included cohabitation with a woman who had very few of the traits I was looking for and compatible with. The predictable result? The relationship ended after we both invested a significant amount of intellectual, emotional and financial capital in a relationship I should have known was doomed from the start. It could have been worse. We almost bought a very expensive house together using my income, credit score and thirty year banking relationship. Thankfully, the lessons I learned by writing this book and this chapter woke me up.

The same is true regarding new jobs or new professional opportunities. Know what you're good at and what the job requirements and each opportunity's success requirements are. If you're not qualified or aren't passionate about the job or opportunity, walk away. The last thing you want to do is to create a self-fulfilling prophecy of predictable professional shit happening and a failure on your resume.

How you deal with the shit that happens in business is equally important as how you deal with the shit that happens in personal relationships. Let's see how you're doing:

1. Think of a recent major setback or shit that happened in your professional life.

2. What happened?

3. Who contributed to it? What was your role?

4. What negative impact did the setback have on the company/you?

5. What could you or others have done to prevent the setback from occurring?

6. Why weren't possible preventive measures

implemented before the setback?

7. What was done to fix the problem/get the company/you back on track?

8. Were all those who created the problem also part of the solution? If not, why not?

9. What happened to all those responsible for the problem and why?

10. What systems, processes, or changes were implemented to prevent a recurrence of the problem?

At Cyberonics, the results of our depression pilot studies suggested that we would have no problem reaching statistical significance in our three-month study that was key to FDA approval. The study was a similar design to the pilot studies but with a control group. The number of centers increased from four to more than twenty.

In classic what-happens-when-you ASS-U-ME, we assumed nothing would go wrong and made an ass out of you (VNS and Cyberonics) and me (every person involved at Cyberonics starting at the top—yours truly). Unfortunately we never discussed what could go wrong, meaning what could cause the acute pivotal study to not reach statistical significance and thereby cause the FDA major heartburn. Had we asked ourselves that simple question, we would have concluded the obvious, which was the treatment group responding significantly worse or the control group responding significantly better in the pivotal study versus the pilot study. Had we then asked ourselves the next logical question, which was what could cause those significant differences in responses, we would have once again concluded the obvious, which was that the treatment group's stimulation dose would be much lower or the control group's stimulation dose would be much higher than the pilot study. Had we come to these two obvious conclusions and asked ourselves how and why these worst-case scenarios could happen we would have considered that in the pivotal study, we had sixteen new centers that had no experience whatsoever with VNS or any other device for that matter. In other words, we would have more carefully trained every one of those new centers and closely monitored all patient stimulation doses to ensure that the study protocol was followed.

Since we used the same instructions to ramp up stimulation parameters to tolerance and provided the same target range for the most efficacious parameters to the depression pivotal study sites as we had used in the pilot studies and in thousands of epilepsy patients, we never imagined that the pivotal study treatment group patients would receive significantly lower levels of stimulation. Which is *exactly* what happened, because we never implemented fixes to prevent the predictable shit that happened. The three-month depression pivotal study, as a result, did not reach statistical significance as expected because the treatment group stimulation parameters were statistically significantly lower than the parameters received by the depression pilot study patients and epilepsy patients treated commercially.

The single biggest issue that the FDA naysayers hung their hats on was our "failed" three-month study. Never mind the one- and two-year results that showed highly significant results with VNS. Never mind that our analyses clearly showed that the pivotal study results were adversely affected by essentially subtherapeutic stimulation parameters. All because we didn't control an easily controlled variable.

When we unblinded our study and were shocked to find that we did not reach statistical significance, we immediately began comprehensive analyses to determine why. Our director of depression studies who was responsible for the conduct of the study argued against any theory other than "shit happens." The more analyses we did, the more he resisted. When it became clear that stimulation parameters were the cause, he refused to acknowledge the data and the only conclusion that could come from the data. He refused to acknowledge that the study sites weren't properly trained. In other words, he refused to take ownership of the problem and his mistakes, which caused the insignificant results. Because he didn't own his mistakes and his share of the major problem that he largely created, he couldn't be part of the solution. As a result, he left the company. Once the stimulation parameters of the three-month pivotal study treatment group patients were turned up in the one- and two-year follow-up, the results were actually better than those of the pilot study patients. The FDA not-approvable crowd obviously didn't care and used our easily explainable, nearly significant "failed" acute study as their reason for destroying the therapy.

My experience tells me that in order for us to master ourselves from the inside out and consistently win when shit happens, we need a simple formula. Here's mine:

1. Identify *all* the predictable shit that might happen in your personal and professional lives and have a plan to prevent it from happening or at least minimize its adverse effects. Much of the shit that happens in our personal and professional lives, whether it be trauma, tragedy, setbacks, suicides, addictions, failures, job losses, financial losses, and divorce is predictable if we rely on all our experience, the experiences of others and the plethora of knowledge available in books.

2. Develop a process to deal with the truly unpredictable shit that happens. Good processes yield good results.

3. Make sure all those who might share in the shit that happens in your life personally and professionally agree with your predictable shit plan and unpredictable shit process discussed above.

4. Pay attention to "devil's advocates" and others who are willing to tell you what you don't want to hear.

5. Don't ass-u-me that shit won't happen to you.

6. Accept that if you don't own the problem, you won't be part of the solution.

7. Accept the fact that unless you own failure, you won't own success.

8. Pay attention to what you're good at, interested in and truly available for in terms of relationships and professional opportunities so that you don't create self-fulfilling prophecies of predictable shit happening.

CHAPTER 11

CAN'T NEVER DID ANYTHING; YOUR DARING GREATLY RECIPE

" Can't never did anything,"--- Grandma Bowie

"It is not the critic who counts; not the man who points out how the strong man stumbles, or where the doer of deeds could have done them better. The credit belongs to the man who is actually in the arena, whose face is marred by dust and sweat and blood; who strives valiantly . . . who knows great enthusiasms, the great devotions; who spends himself in a worthy cause; who at the best knows in the end the triumph of high achievement, and who at the worst, if he fails, at least fails while daring greatly, so that his place shall never be with those cold and timid souls who neither know victory nor defeat." —Theodore Roosevelt

---

WHICH OF THE following messages do you read into Theodore Roosevelt's quote?

1. Critics are focused on the past?

2. Doers that dare greatly, with enthusiasm and devotion, are focused on the present and future?

3. Critics are afraid of mistakes and failures?

4. Cold and timid souls who know neither victory nor defeat never dare greatly because they are afraid of mistakes and failures?

5. Doers who dare greatly, by definition, have worthy causes and/or big dreams? Critics do not?

6. Doers who dare greatly know that mistakes and failures, victories and defeats, are inevitable when daring greatly?

7. Doers who dare greatly embrace mistakes and failures and learn from them so that the next time they dare greatly, their chances of success are greater?

Based on your interpretation of the above quote, and your experience, which are you? Critic or doer? Are you afraid of mistakes and failures or do you accept that mistakes/failures are inevitable when learning, growing, and daring greatly? Do you embrace and learn from mistakes/failures or do you run and hide from them? Or blame others for them? Are you inspiring/enabling those around you to be critics or doers who dare greatly? Do the rewards for success that you've created for yourself and those around you, including those you manage at work, your kids, etc., sufficiently outweigh the consequences of mistakes and failures such that you and those around you are motivated to dare greatly?

Here's an excercise to help you determine if you're a doer, a critic or both.

1. What worthy causes or big dreams have justified you daring greatly, striving valiantly, and exhausting yourself to achieve?

2. Describe a time when you were a doer, dared greatly, ignored a large number of critics, and were successful. How did you define success? What made you successful? Who were the critics and what were they saying? What were your rewards for daring greatly, ignoring the critics, and being successful?

3. Describe a time when you were a doer, dared greatly, ignored a large number of critics, and weren't successful. How did you define success? Why did you fail? Did you own/embrace and learn from your mistakes? Did your mistakes/ failure cause you to become more of a reticent doer and less willing to dare greatly? How did you successfully apply what you learned from your mistakes/failure to future situations?

4. Describe a time when you listened to the critics, including your inner critic, and didn't dare greatly. What was the outcome of your decision? Are you happy with your decision and its outcome? If not, what could you have done differently to create a more positive outcome?

5. What is your formula to inspire yourself and those around you to be doers who dare greatly?

My recipe to dare greatly and make big dreams a reality was originally inspired by two of Grandma Bowie's favorite sayings: "You'll never know where you stand from where you sit" and "Can't never did anything." Over the ensuing fifty-five or so years, my recipe has evolved and been applied first unconsciously, then increasingly consciously to inspire myself and others. My recipe now has six key ingredients: (1) dream big, (2) create a plan consisting of a series of small doable steps to make the big dream a reality, (3) create significant incentives for accomplishment of each step, such that the likelihood of achieving and the magnitude of the incentives far outweigh the risks and cost of mistakes and failure, (4) "get after it" with passion and commitment, (5) use the critics as fuel for success, and (6) "compassionate accountability."

The first of the key ingredients in my formula to dare greatly is to dream big—however you define "dream" and "big." We all have different definitions. For me, all dreams are by definition big, otherwise they wouldn't be dreams. I dreamed of being an NFL quarterback like Bart Starr of the Green Bay Packers. I dreamed of getting out of the small town in western Pennsylvania where I was born. I dreamed of playing college football. I dreamed of being the first person from my small town to graduate from an Ivy League school. I dreamed of being a scuba diver and skier. I dreamed of becoming a venture capitalist. I dreamed of improving the lives of hundreds of thousands of people touched by treatment-resistant illnesses. I dreamed of being a good husband and father and creating a happy, healthy, and successful family. I dreamed of commercializing the first FDA-approved treatment for severe depression and giving people like my mother an option other than suicide. I dreamed of being "somebody" who made a huge positive difference in the world around me. I dreamed of being regarded as a successful person who earned everything he has in life and did things the right way. My current dream is to use this book and all my experience, knowledge, and wisdom, including my successes, mistakes, and failures, to improve people's lives. Including yours.

Big dreams create big rewards and minimal expectations from the "legion of can't." Most in the legion expect you to fail or make mistakes in your pursuit of your big dreams. Don't try to convince them otherwise and raise their expectations. Let the rewards for making your dreams a reality far exceed the costs of the expected failures or mistakes. Isn't accomplishing 10%, 25%, 50% of a big dream better than never trying and becoming "can't never did anything" incarnate? From a pure risk-and-return perspective, the answer is always yes. So why not dream big and give it a shot?

The second key ingredient is to create a step-by-step plan of relatively small, doable steps to make your big dream a reality. Many times while helicopter skiing and at Cyberonics, the impossible became the possible with a step-by-step plan. I can remember standing at the top of a fifteen-foot cornice leading to an incredibly steep, 6,000 vertical foot, rarely skied run in the Bugaboos called Anniversary Chute, thinking to myself, "Wow, this is a *really* long, *really* steep run. If I fall it won't be good. How am I going to do this?" On a snowboard no less, which I only learned to ride two months prior! I knew the longer I waited and debated the worse it would be, so I simultaneously said to myself, "One turn at a time," jumped off the cornice, and made one turn at a time, fell, and slid 2,500 vertical feet; got up and made one turn at a time for 3,500 vertical feet down to the waiting helicopter. As I climbed in I looked up at the run and thought, "How in god's name did I do that?" One turn at a time. Including a very scary fall and a 2,500 vertical foot high-speed slide. Perfect metaphor for daring greatly.

Similarly at Cyberonics, we were trying to do something no one had ever done before. Such as overturning a not-approvable letter that, upon receipt, appeared to be a completely impossible task. The "legion of can't" outside the company knew we couldn't do it and expected us to fail, and many inside Cyberonics were paralyzed by fear. Perfect. No expectations meaning no costs associated with failure. Huge rewards for success. All we had to do was develop a plan of small steps that everyone inside Cyberonics believed were doable, the most difficult and frightening of which, as CEO, I agreed to do. And suddenly we were "daring greatly" so that, at worst, if we failed, our places would never be with those "cold and timid souls who neither know victory nor defeat."

The third key ingredient in my recipe for making big dreams a reality is to create bonuses or rewards for the accomplishment of each of the small "doable" steps in the plan. At Cyberonics, the incentives and rewards for attempting the impossible and overcoming the inertia of can't were well known—cash and stock bonuses and stock price appreciation. However, in many cases, those incentives need to be created for yourself or for others, such as your kids to inspire yourself and them to "dare greatly."

Have you ever used "bonuses" as incentives to get your kids focused on the "prize"? I have, with great success. With both my veterinarian daughter and my University of Texas football player son, I used financial incentives to motivate them to get the best grades possible. Each semester, starting in ninth grade, I paid them a $100 bonus for an A, and a $50 bonus for a B. If they had all As the amount they earned was tripled. If they had an A average, the amount they earned was doubled. If they had a D, they forfeited everything they otherwise earned in that semester. If they had an F, they forfeited everything they otherwise earned in that semester and paid me $1,000.

The bonus plan totally focused them on realizing their potential instead of being afraid of making a mistake. Prior to the bonus plan being implemented, neither of them ever had a D or F, so the costs and risks of those failures didn't scare them. Instead, they were motivated to get all As or at least an A average that would earn them bonuses for each semester of $2,100 and $1,400, respectively. I don't recall many semesters when they didn't earn at least $1,400. The bonuses my son and daughter earned could then be saved or spent on whatever they wanted, within reason. But an effective incentive doesn't have to be money; it could be tickets to a concert, a day at an amusement park, a new phone, new clothes. The key is that the bonuses were meaningful and the upside of daring greatly and accomplishing their goals far outweighed the risks and costs of failing or making a mistake.

As my daughter's and son's dreams changed to include goals like having a car and being accepted and going to the college of their choice, their bonus plans continued to focus them on daring greatly instead of listening to the critics. My daughter earned her first car by getting straight As and an almost perfect score on the SAT while developing and maintaining a positive social life and a variety of nonacademic interests, including skiing, horseback riding, and dance. My son earned the right to drive my Ford F-150 pickup as if it were his own at age sixteen based on good grades, outstanding performance in football, doing his jobs at home, being respectful, and staying out of trouble.

After the fall semester of his junior year, my son decided that in order to realize his dream of playing major college football, he needed to transfer from his small private school in Austin whose football program he had outgrown to a private school in Fort Worth that every year had three or more football players receive full scholarships to a Division 1 school. He also really wanted a new truck. When he wanted to leave his girlfriend, his friends, and a school where he was a "BMOC" (big man on campus) academically, socially, and athletically and transfer to a new high school where he'd need to prove himself all over again, I knew he was committed to daring greatly to make his big dreams a reality. All I had to do was help him create a step-by-step plan and bonuses to reward him for achieving his goals.

His bonuses included monthly bonuses and a new truck in

the spring of his senior year based on implementation of his plan both in terms of timing and achievement of his goals for grades, his SAT score, extracurricular and volunteer activities, football performance, and promoting his football "brand" to obtain full scholarship offers. A new truck was a great deal for both of us. He had all the incentive he needed to achieve his full scholarship goal and if he achieved that goal, a new truck would cost me less than 35% of a four-year college education without a scholarship. The plan to get full scholarship offers included developing a list of target schools, going to those schools' summer camps before his senior year, regularly communicating with the appropriate coaches at those target schools, creating and distributing highlight films for every game, regularly tweeting his academic and football accomplishments to his 1,500 or so followers, and, of course, staying out of trouble. Although he was a complete unknown after his junior season at the small private school in Austin, he diligently implemented his plan and not only did he get full scholarship offers from schools like Oklahoma, University of Texas, and Baylor, but he earned a new Ford F-250 pickup that he "leases" from me, his lease payments being good grades, good football performance, and him staying out of trouble at the University of Texas where he is now a student getting a "free" education thanks to his full football scholarship. Note that his full scholarship, which he is earning by "working" an average of four to six hours a day year round for UT football, is saving me over $200,000 in education costs!

So what bonus plans have you created for yourself to dare greatly and accomplish the series of small steps that will make your big dreams a reality?

Whenever you've made mistakes or failed to accomplish a goal in the past, what do you think caused those mistakes or failures? Have you ever attributed your mistake or failure to inadequate effort or simply not working hard enough? Make a list of five things you need to do to be a successful parent, a good spouse, successful in your job, etc., and give each of those five things a degree of difficulty from one to three, three being the most difficult. Isn't working hard and making maximum effort the easiest of those tasks?

My fourth key ingredient for making big dreams a reality is passion and commitment that yield maximum effort and cause us to work both harder and smarter. Without passion and commitment, you are wasting your time, which is why the greatest gift I ever hoped to receive from my kids was them finding their passion. Every time we work harder and smarter than we thought possible, don't we prove to everyone around us—most importantly ourselves—that there is no limit to how hard we can and will work and that hard work won't kill us? In Grove City, by the time I was in junior high, I knew that I was going places not because I was the biggest, strongest, smartest, most athletic kid around, which I wasn't, but because I had bigger dreams and I was willing to outwork all the bigger, stronger, smarter kids to make my dreams a reality. I would sooner die than quit. And being called a quitter was at the top of my list of fighting words.

High school football in a small town in western Pennsylvania in the late '60s and early '70s was definitely "old school." And the perfect place for me to prove to myself and others that nobody would outwork me. Dirt practice field. Three practices a day during preseason training camp in eighty-five degree heat and 80% humidity. No water breaks except being hosed down like cattle. No such thing as Gatorade. Grueling conditioning drills.

One evening at the end of a two-hour practice (our third two-hour practice of the day in the same filthy, soaked-with-sweat jockstrap and uniform) our coaches decided that we should do one-hundred grass drills, i.e., run in place, and when the coach blew the whistle, dive on the ground, then jump back up with legs pumping, and repeat a hundred times. Unfortunately, I had eaten a spaghetti dinner before practice, so at about grass drill number eighty with legs pumping, I vomited half-digested spaghetti and garlic bread on the ground in front of me. The whistle blew, I dove on the ground, and jumped back up with legs pumping wearing a jersey now covered with spaghetti sauce, chunks of spaghetti, and garlic bread. At the end of practice, neither my coaches, nor my teammates, nor I could believe what I did. But, when the going gets tough, the tough get going, especially when it comes to jumping in your own vomit. Point made. Most importantly to myself.

Sounds silly, but that's the same philosophy I've applied throughout my life to make sure that hard work didn't scare me and "my boss" knew I would outwork everyone. My "boss" often being myself and my inner critic, who often tried to take over. During summer breaks at Dartmouth and in business school, I worked construction to pay for school. On my first day on the job during graduate school in Champaign, Illinois, we were pouring new concrete aprons at the local airport. We started at 7:00 a.m. because it was supposed to be over ninety degrees with over 85% humidity. Being my first day, I naturally wanted to prove to all my coworkers that I belonged, so I didn't pace myself. Everything I did was maximum effort. All day I stood in and shoveled wet concrete some two-feet deep. With my BA from Dartmouth. Thinking it was lunchtime, I looked at my watch and it was only 9:30 a.m. After lunch, I cramped every time I moved. I probably drank and perspired five gallons of water. When one of the other laborers complained to the superintendent that it was brutally hot, the super got out of his air-conditioned Lincoln and hosed us down using the hose on the concrete truck. Our workday was finally done at about 5:00 p.m. I walked, maybe trudged or stumbled are better words, back to my car more exhausted than I had ever been with concrete burns all over my arms and legs, and inner thighs so badly chafed they were bleeding. I laid next to my car and fell asleep for a few hours until after dark, when I awoke with the realization that most if not all union laborers I was working with were betting that the Dartmouth football player getting his MBA wouldn't show up the next day. On my drive home, I analyzed the mistakes I made and what I could have done differently that day to make it less painful.

Good thing my coworkers didn't bet on me quitting, because I was back in the concrete at 7:00 a.m. the next morning. Once again, point made. Most importantly to myself. But also to my coworkers and boss who had newfound respect for me. At this point, you may be thinking, "Yes, Skip, you worked hard shoveling that concrete, but you didn't work smart." I agree and, like you, believe that working hard also means working smarter every day to maximize your productivity. I never again ate a spaghetti dinner before an evening football practice and the next day and everyday after shoveling concrete, I paced myself and wore gloves and a long-sleeved shirt, all of which enabled me to be more consistently productive throughout ensuing practices and work days.

Had I not learned from my mistakes and continued to work harder, not smarter, I would have been like the young man who was hired to chop down a forest of trees with his ax. An old man who had cut down more than his fair share of trees watched him for almost an entire day. Toward the end of the day, the old man walked up to the profusely sweating, obviously exhausted young man with bleeding hands and said to him, "You know, you might be able to cut those trees down faster if you stop and sharpen your ax," to which the young man replied, "I can't. I'm too busy cutting down these trees." In other words, "I'm too busy working hard to work smart."

Grueling football practices and long painful days shoveling concrete gave me the confidence, strength, passion, and commitment to lead by example, consistently work over ninety-hour weeks, dare greatly, and overcome one seemingly impossible challenge after another at Cyberonics to pioneer and commercialize new medical science and revolutionary new device-based therapy.

The fifth key ingredient in my daring greatly formula is to use the critics as fuel for success. The best way to do this is to first consider your critics' potential impact on whatever it is you're trying to accomplish, then consider their relevant knowledge and experience, and finally their agenda (reason for their criticism). What I learned the hard way, contrary to the Theodore Roosevelt quote in which he says that critics don't count, is that all critics are not created equal. Some don't have any impact on whatever it is you're trying to accomplish and no relevant knowledge or experience. These critics, as a result, don't count—meaning they should be ignored or dismissed so they don't become a distraction. Some, however, do count in that they can affect the outcome of whatever it is you're trying to do or they have relevant knowledge and experience. These critics, depending on their agenda, can provide you with valuable information for your daring greatly journey. The trick is to figure out which are which.

My track record using critics as fuel for success as opposed to mistakes and failures isn't great, but it's getting better given what I know now. At times I chose to allow critics to distract me from whatever it was I was daring greatly to do and focus my efforts on proving them wrong. At times I chose to allow critics to cause me to do things that were clearly not in my best interest. At times I ignored critics who had no agenda other than sharing with me their relevant knowledge and experience. The critics I have and continue to encounter seem to fit into the following categories:

1. **The Can't-Never-Did-Anything Critics:** These critics are so afraid of trying anything new that they keep doing the same things over and over. These critics are genuinely afraid for themselves and you.

2. **Your-Failures-Are-Their-Successes Critics:** There seem to be an awful lot of these in America today. Critics whose lives are zero-sum games in which they only win what you lose and whose success in life comes only from others' failures.

3. **Victim Critics:** These critics think that the only reason they're not successful is because of what someone or something did to them. Heaven forbid that you are successful under similar circumstances.

4. **For-Profit Critics:** These critics get paid in some way to be critics. There are many for-profit critics in the media, on Wall Street, in politics. Negativity, controversy, vilification, fear, and someone else's failure generate significant profits for these critics.

5. **Inner Critic:** This is the most influential and dangerous of the masters of "can't." Because this critic is YOU. The critic inside you who pretends he or she is only looking out for your best interests and feels a need to protect you from more mistakes and failures that this critic can't tolerate.

What impact have critics, including your inner critic, had on your life? Thinking back, have they caused you to doubt yourself and convinced you that you can't do something that you wished you had "dared greatly" and tried to do? Have they distracted you from whatever it was you were daring greatly to do? Don't your critics, especially your inner critic, constantly remind you of past mistakes and failures to scare you out of "daring greatly"? So how do you motivate yourself and those around you to ignore critics, including inner critics, risk mistakes and failures, and dare greatly?

While writing this book in California and observing differences in California versus Texas parenting, I uncovered a sixth key ingredient to making big dreams a reality. It's an oxymoron called "compassionate accountability." Compassion is defined by *Merriam-Webster* as "sympathetic consciousness of others' distress with a desire to alleviate it." Accountability is the "state of being responsible and held to account for one's actions." Compassion seems to be universally viewed as a positive trait. Holding someone accountable, not so much. Especially in California. I have watched many professionals, parents, and people in general experience a lot of angst holding themselves, other adults, and their children accountable. It seems as though our natural inclination when someone is struggling is to be what we think is compassionate and give them a break. Meaning accommodate, indulge, and/or in some way reward what could be poor choices, a lack of integrity, bad behavior, or nonperformance, including failures to respect previously agreed to boundaries, honor promises and commitments, and implement previously agreed to plans.

But is accommodating, indulging, or rewarding behavior or nonperformance compassionate? It may be "sympathetic consciousness of others' distress" but it shows no "desire to alleviate" that stress if stress is defined as failure to implement the plan that will make their big dreams a reality. Why dream big, create a plan consisting of small, doable steps, and reward achievement for completing those small doable steps unless you're going to hold yourself and others accountable? Isn't making the big dream a reality the goal? Won't failure to make that dream a reality cause distress? If so, then to be compassionate, you must hold yourself and others accountable.

A perfect example of the importance of compassionate accountability is my son's ninth grade academic improvement plan. He created a plan to get his grades and GPA up consistent with past performance. His plan called for him to change several inputs, including going to at least two tutoring sessions with two teachers each week, eliminating all TV and video games during the week, doing all weekend homework and semester to date reviews of each of his subjects on Saturday before any social-izing, and sending a weekly grades spreadsheet to his mother and me before he left school on Fridays. So what happened if he only went to one tutoring session, didn't finish his weekend work before going out, forgot to send us his grades spreadsheet, etc.? The first time, *if* he had a reasonable explanation, we let it go. The second time, because it was *his* plan to change *his* inputs to increase *his* GPA to where *he* wanted it, we exercised compas-sionate accountability and he lost phone or social privileges for a day or two. The loss of privileges increased with his failures to implement *his* plan. He didn't necessarily see our holding him accountable as being compassionate but when he predictably didn't lose many privileges, his grades and GPA went up and he earned a larger cash bonus, he thanked us for our help.

I've always been a process person, meaning I believe that good processes produce good results and bad processes produce bad results. I now know that I have a process, formula, recipe to inspire people, including myself to dream big, dare greatly, and make dreams a reality. It worked for many at Cyberonics. My formula worked for my young adult children. And it's working for me as evidenced by me ignoring all the critics, most importantly my inner critic, and writing this book. All it takes is a step-by-step plan and incentives and rewards that far outweigh the costs or consequences of inevitable mistakes and failures, learning how to use critics as fuel for success, and compassionate accountability. Can't never did anything and it's not the critic who counts, only those that dare greatly, according to Grandma Bowie and Teddy Roosevelt.

Next time you or those around you, including your kids or coworkers, have a dream, give your version of my daring greatly formula a try. What do you have to lose? At worst, if you fail, at least you'll know that your place will never be with those "cold and timid souls who neither know victory nor defeat."

CHAPTER 12

HOW TO DELIVER ON YOUR PROMISES AND BE A HERO

"If you overpromise and underdeliver you're a bum. If you underpromise and overdeliver you're a hero. Even if you deliver the same thing in each case."—Anonymous

SHORTLY AFTER I joined Continental Bank's venture capital subsidiary, I had dinner with a CEO who had built a very successful computer memory company (remember hard and floppy disk drives?). I asked him about the single most important thing he wished he had done differently. His answer? Better managed expectations by consistently underpromising and overdelivering. He then told me the story, probably true of a CEO who promised 50% sales growth in one year and only delivered 35% sales growth to $135 million. Because the CEO overpromised and under delivered, he was regarded by his board, investors, and others as a failure (a bum) even though sales increased 35%. A different CEO of a similar company with $100 million in sales promised sales growth of 25%, but delivered 30% sales growth to $130 million. Even though his company's sales were less than those of the CEO who was considered a failure, this CEO was considered to be a success because he overdelivered. The difference between being considered a bum and a hero being whether or not you over or underdeliver on your promises.

Here are a few questions your answers to which will help you determine if you are a hero or bum as regards your promises:

1. How often do you deliver on your promises? Always? Most of the time? Sometimes? Rarely? Never?

2. How often would your boss say that you deliver on your promises? Write down one or two promises that you've recently made to your boss on which you've delivered. Same for one or two promises on which you didn't deliver. What were the rewards and consequences in each case? What were the causes of your failure to deliver? How did you feel about delivering and not delivering on your promises? What did you learn from your failures to deliver?

3. How often would your spouse/significant other say you deliver on your promises? Write down one or two promises that you've recently made to your spouse/significant other on which you've delivered. Same for one or two promises on which you didn't deliver. What were the rewards and consequences in each case? What were the causes of your failure to deliver? How did you feel about delivering and not delivering on your promises? What did you learn from your failures to deliver?

4. How often would your children say that you

deliver on your promises? Answer the same questions here that you did in number three substituting your children for your spouse/ significant other.

5. How often would your professional peers say that you deliver on your promises? Answer the same questions listed above **in number 1**, substituting peers for boss.

6. How often would those who report to you at work say that you deliver on your promises? Answer the same questions listed **above in #1**, substituting those who report to you for boss.

7. Write down two promises you recently made to yourself that you've delivered on. Same for one or two promises on which you didn't deliver. What were the rewards and consequences in each case? What were the causes of your failure to deliver? How did you feel about delivering and not delivering on your promises to yourself? What did you learn from your failures to deliver?

Doesn't your answer to the questions regarding how often you deliver on your promises depend on what you consider to be a "promise?" What is a promise? Is a promise limited only to those things that you specifically promise to do by saying something like, "I *promise* to be home **at five**?" If so, how about all the other things you say you'll do without using the word "promise"? Such as, "I'll be home **at five**." Or the things you say you'll do with qualifications or conditions? Such as, "I'll try to be home **by five**," or, "My intention is to home **by five**," or "Maybe I'll be home by five," or "I plan to be home at five."

So let's say that in answering the previous questions you discover that you have promises, will dos, and maybe dos. To what standards do you hold yourself in terms of delivering on your promises, will dos, and maybe dos? What percent of the time do you hold yourself accountable for delivering on your promises? On your will dos? On your maybe dos? Promises at least 90% of the time? Will dos a lower percentage, such as at least 70% of the time? And maybe dos the lowest percentage, such as at least 25% of the time? Make sense?

Before we continue, let's consider all those people to whom we make promises, communicate will dos, and share maybe dos. My list is a very long list. How about yours? You probably make promises, communicate will dos, and express maybe dos to yourself, your significant other, your children, your family, your friends, acquaintances, your bank, your landlord, and professionally to hundreds of people you work with, including your boss, peers, subordinates, customers, suppliers, lawyers, investors, banks, and various governmental agencies.

If we go back to what the CEO of the computer memory company told me, underpromising and overdelivering is a means to an effective expectations management end. And that effective expectations management is critical to being and being considered successful. In other words, to master ourselves from the inside out and be a successful person personally and professionally, we need to be careful about the expectations we create in ourselves and others so that we meet or exceed those expectations by delivering on our promises.

How in the world are you going to effectively manage the expectations of all those to whom you make promises, communicate will dos, and express maybe dos if you intend to deliver on your promises 90% of the time, your will dos 75% of the time, and maybe dos 25% of the time? Even if you were able to inform everyone on your list about your definitions of promises, will dos, and maybe dos and how often they should expect you to deliver on each, how will those on your list know the difference between specific promises, will dos, and maybe dos they should expect you to deliver on? The answer is they can't and won't. Therefore, your definitions of promises, will dos?

To consistently deliver on our promises, perhaps we need a much simpler definition of a promise. If promises create expectations, aren't promises anything we say or do that creates an expectation in ourselves or others? In other words, it's not what we actually say or do that constitutes an expectations-creating promise, but rather what others *hear* us say or see us do that they perceive to be a promise. Others' perceptions thus become our promises' reality. Such that, consistent with what the computer memory CEO told me, if we underdeliver on those perceived promises in the extreme, we're a bum. If we overdeliver, we're a hero.

What do you think of people who consistently deliver on their promises? Aren't they the same people who mean what they say and do, and vice versa? The same people who "walk their talk"? Do you regard them as dependable? Trustworthy? Someone you want to be around or work with? Someone who makes a positive difference and adds value to the world? If so, one of the many traits of successful people, personally and professionally, is that they consistently deliver on the promises that their words and deeds create in the minds of others. A promise kept and expectation met is indeed a positive for everyone.

The mother of my children and wife of twenty-one years taught me the importance of delivering or overdelivering on every promise that children, especially your own, perceive that you made to them. My tantra training and practice taught me that as parents, we create the environment from whence our children come and are therefore responsible for their thoughts, feelings, fears, and triggers as adults. Children need to know that their parents love, approve, and support them. Children also need to know that they are high priorities for their parents. Promises kept give children of all ages that knowledge. Promises broken make children feel unimportant, like their needs don't matter and, in the extreme, abandoned. Been there experienced that.

Every promise your children perceive you to make to them is a big deal. If children can't trust and depend on their parents, who can they trust and depend on? And children of all ages have a funny way of considering even the most conditioned statements as promises. If you tell your son or daughter that you'll "try," that "maybe," or that you "plan" to be home from work at a certain time to go swimming, play catch with the football, or go to one of their school functions, do you think they heard the words *try, maybe,* or *plan*? Or do you think they heard you promise and therefore expect you to be home from work at a certain time and do that something with them? How do you think your son or daughter feels if, for whatever reason, you're not home at that certain time and don't do that certain something they heard you promise to do? How about if you are home at that certain time but don't do that certain something with them? Even if you called ahead and gave them the reason? Do you think they feel like they're important and a high priority for you? Or do you think they'll feel like their needs don't matter? And if you regularly fail to deliver on what they perceive to be your promises, at what point do your children conclude once and for all that you only love and care about them if and when they fit into your otherwise busy schedule?

There are many ways and places for your children to find the love and validation they need. Wouldn't you rather that validation come from you at home? If so, why not follow the advice of the

computer memory CEO and better manage your children's expectations by consistently underpromising and overdelivering. In
other words, refrain from making statements that your children
will hear as promises unless you are certain that you will deliver
on them. Instead of using phrases like "I'll try," "maybe," or "I
plan to," and risking their feelings by creating a promise you're
not confident you'll keep, why not keep quiet then surprise them?
Meaning make no explicit or implicit promise, then overdeliver?
Better a hero than a bum, especially to your kids. The same goes
for your significant other and everyone else with whom you have
a personal or professional relationship.

Another important reason to deliver on promises you make
to your children is the example you're setting and the lessons
you're teaching them about the promises they make to you and
the promises they will one day make to their significant other
and children. Can you think of a perceived promise that you were
surprised to learn others firmly believed they heard you make?
I can think of several that may help you.

As chairman and CEO of Cyberonics, I regularly communicated with many people whose support I needed to be
successful, including the board of directors, employees and
their families, investors, the media, analysts, neurologists and
psychiatrists, nurses, patients and their families, insurance
companies, the FDA, lawyers, investment bankers, plus my wife,
my children, our friends. What people *heard* me say or not say
often created as many if not more promises and expectations
than what I actually said.

Our policy at Cyberonics was to tell investors what they
needed to know to make fully informed investment decisions.
Unfortunately that policy created many situations in which
we were perceived as having overpromised and underdeliv-
ered regarding FDA approval, insurance coverage, and sales,

especially considering that the only comparable precedent we had in depression was what happened with our device in epilepsy. When we provided investors with the epilepsy timeline for FDA approval, they assumed it would be similar for depression and we would get FDA approval shortly after the favorable panel vote.

When we actually received a not-approvable letter, investors were livid that we—specifically I—didn't deliver on what they perceived to be our/my promises. I was a bum for overpromising and underdelivering. When we justified our significant investment in our depression studies and expanded sales force by informing investors that there were ten times the number of patients with treatment-resistant depression as there were with refractory epilepsy, despite our conservative guidance to the contrary, they extrapolated those patient numbers to mean we were promising that depression sales would be ten times those of epilepsy. When we exceeded our formal guidance but failed to deliver on what investors perceived to be a promise that justified their extrapolated expectations, I was once again a bum. It was a similar situation when it came to insurance coverage by the major payers. We provided investors with conservative formal guidance that we exceeded. However, we also provided them with the epilepsy coverage timeline and all the reasons that we were in a better position to obtain coverage in depression. Once again, investors extrapolated the depression versus epilepsy comparison to create expectations for coverage in depression that, when not met, confirmed I was an overpromising and underdelivering bum. On each of these failures to deliver, our stock took a big hit, causing all shareholders, including the most supportive shareholders, to wonder if I was more trouble than I was worth.

These failures to properly manage expectations and over-deliver on what investors perceived to be my promises no doubt contributed to my demise at Cyberonics. When the FDA not-approvable crowd, the Senate Finance Committee, SunTrust, Wall Street, the SEC, and the media came after me personally, what little support I still had quickly ran for cover. I was an over-promising, underdelivering bum involved in FDA-approval and stock-option improprieties who needed to be disposed of as quickly as possible. Never mind that the allegations were false. Completely false. If I only knew then what I know now.

Have I convinced you yet of the importance of carefully managing personal and professional expectations by being conscious of the promises you are perceived to be making to those with whom you have a personal or professional relationship? Think about the last time you failed to deliver on a promise, do what you said you'd do, or do what someone thought you'd promised to do. How did the person to whom you made that promise feel? Surprised? Disappointed? Unimportant? Angry? Sad? What ripple effects did your failure to deliver on your promise have on those interacting with that person? How did you feel? Embarrassed? Defensive? Unconcerned? Apologetic? Determined to not break another promise? Did the person who felt the impact of your broken promise say something to you? Did you apologize?

Think also about a specific instance when someone failed to deliver on what you perceived to be a personal or professional promise and repeatedly failed to deliver on what you perceived to a personal or professional promise. How did you feel? How did your opinion of them change? If they lost credibility with you, how long did it take them to earn that credibility back?

Unfortunately those whom you've disappointed often don't express that disappointment or let you know that you've failed to deliver on what they perceived to be one or more of your promises. Or let you know that you've failed to deliver so many times that they don't trust you and can't count on or depend on you.

Unless we are conscious of and sensitive to the expectations we're creating and promises we are perceived to be making, we are at risk of doing irreparable damage to the relationships that are most important to us. Unfortunately when it comes to broken promises and promises that we failed to deliver on, many times there are no do-overs. What's done is done, which is one of the many things I know now about promises that I wish I knew then.

What does more damage to a relationship, failing to deliver on a "difficult" promise or failing to deliver on an "easy" promise? Let's say you promise your family that you're going to get a big bonus and when you do, you're going to take them to Maui on vacation. Something totally out of your control, such as the company cancelling all bonuses, prevents you from delivering the promised Maui vacation. You and your family are disappointed that you failed to deliver on your promise but everyone understands that you did everything in your power to do so.

Now let's look at an "easy" promise. Let's say you're doing a six-month consulting project that requires you to be in another state five days a week. You promise to call your spouse and daughter every night, and you deliver on that promise for the first three months. Then, without any explanation, you start calling or texting them every other night, then every third night. When your spouse shares her and your daughter's hurt feelings with you, you rationalize your failure to call as being tired, at the gym, or watching football. What message are you sending to your family by failing to deliver on this "easy" promise? That they're not important enough to talk to every night for ten to twenty minutes as you did in the past? That what's happening in their lives isn't a high priority for you? That you don't have time in your busy schedule or miss them enough to hear their voices and tell them you love them? For me, I know now that nothing hurts more than someone failing to deliver on an "easy" promise.

So what about promises we make to ourselves? Aren't these some of the most important promises, given that whether we deliver on them largely determines how much we respect ourselves, how important we think we are to ourselves, and how high a priority we put on ourselves? If we don't have the discipline and consciousness to manage our own expectations and make promises to ourselves that we keep, how can we expect to deliver on our promises and effectively manage the expectations we create in others?

Think about the last promise you made to yourself that you kept and the last promise you failed to keep. How did you feel in each of those instances? If we believe that every promise, big and small, matters, then we need to be as careful about making perceived promises to ourselves as we are in making perceived promises to, and creating expectations in, others.

In my case, since I started working on this book, I have repeatedly promised myself and my book and business consultant that I would carve out four hours a day to focus on writing. Until recently, I have chosen to be distracted by what should be lower priorities, and comfortable overpromising and underdelivering to myself! Not anymore. My wake-up call came in the form of a detailed plan and timeline to not only complete and publish this book, but also build my brand and business as a speaker, online teacher, and coach/confidante, helping others master themselves from the inside out by first mastering myself from the inside out, using everything I know now that I wish I knew then. I'm now back on track and firmly committed to delivering on my promises to myself and to those who might benefit from this book. Needless to say, this chapter also enlightened me to the fact that when promises aren't kept, everyone involved is adversely affected.

Now that I've shared my experience with promises and under and overdelivering on promises, go back and re-answer the questions I asked you at the beginning of this chapter. Are your answers different? If so, how? As is the case with many of the chapters in this book, learning how to consistently deliver on your promises aned holding yourself compassionately account-able are a key ingredients to mastering you from the inside out, creating extraordinary relationships with yourself and others, and realizing your full potential.

CHAPTER 13

SELLING AND BUYING YOUR WAY TO ABUNDANCE

Everyone is selling something. Abundance comes from being a great salesperson and an astute buyer.

ROBERT LOUIS STEVENSON, author of *Treasure Island* and *The Strange Case of Dr. Jekyll and Mr. Hyde*, once said, "Everybody lives by selling something." Good advice regarding the importance of being a good salesperson. How about advice regarding being an astute buyer? In the late middle ages, the expression "don't buy a pig in a poke" came from people being duped into buying what they believed to be a pig, a good source of meat but scarce at the time, in a bag ("poke") when, in reality, inside the bag was a cat or dog, which were plentiful. It's interesting to note that the expression "let the cat out of the bag" came from the same practice as did the Latin term *caveat emptor*, or "buyer beware."

In the 1920s, the expression about buying or being sold "a bill of goods" first appeared, in which "bill of goods" means a dishonest offer that's intended to deceive, swindle, or take unfair advantage of a gullible buyer. "A fool and his money will soon be parted" is an old English proverb that emphasizes the importance of being an astute buyer to preserve abundance. "Buy low, sell high" is another expression that emphasizes the importance of being an astute buyer, then seller.

Robert Louis Stevenson would be shocked by today's definitions of "everybody" and "something" in his quote "Everybody lives by selling something." The "something" that everybody is trying to sell includes ideas, opinions, cars, houses, clothes, vacations, entertainment, meals at certain restaurants, charitable and political contributions, elective surgery, weight-loss programs, gym memberships, spa services, some sort of relationship with another person, concepts. "Everybody" includes your family, friends, car salespeople, real estate agents, your boss, peers and subordinates at work, doctors, lawyers, neighbors, ubiquitous—and I mean ubiquitous—advertising, celebrities, Amazon, retail stores and the people who work there, billboards. Everywhere we turn, almost every person we interact with, and almost everything we see or hear is trying to sell us something, or perhaps said in a better way, trying to convince us to buy something.

In the old days, we used to send friends letters to let them know how we were doing. Then emails. Sometimes with photos attached. No advertisers or anyone trying to sell us something could access those letters or emails for targeted marketing. Not until Facebook appeared and replaced letters and emails. Facebook enabled us to tell everyone everything about ourselves. Simultaneously. Online. If you've ever wondered why the Facebook ads that appear on your timeline seem relevant, and if you've ever advertised on Facebook like I have, you know that Facebook makes its money by selling highly targeted advertising based on all the personal information it collects without paying you anything.

Another challenge of being an astute, well-informed buyer in today's world is that much of what we buy today is not a single purchase but a monthly subscription. In the old days, we used to buy a one or two annual magazine subscriptions. Now, you probably buy subscriptions that hit your credit card every month until canceled. Your first month is often free, then you pay every month until you cancel. Cancelling is not easy. In most cases, you can't cancel online. You have to call and actually get a human being on the phone. Predictably, the waits are long to reach a human being who can cancel your subscription. Take a look at your credit card bills and see how many subscriptions you're paying for and actually using! Probably less than half.

Given that we are being sold something almost every second of every day, and many of those somethings are monthly subscriptions, in today's world a fool and his money will soon, as in real-time, be parted. Never before has being an astute, well-informed buyer been more important to accumulating and preserving abundance of all kinds. Let's see how you're doing in terms of being an astute buyer.

1. Think about a couple of tangible things that you were recently convinced to buy outside of work that cost you a significant amount of money. New house, car, investment, phone, TV, computer, furniture, clothes, etc. One purchase that you were totally happy with. Another that caused you to have buyer's remorse. What were the causes of your buyer's remorse? Did you pay too much? Were you get in a hurry and bought before you'd done all your research? Did you buy a want instead of a need? Were you a fully informed buyer? Did you know exactly what you were paying, such as a one-time amount or a monthly subscription? Did the salesperson

who sold you whatever it is you bought seem committed to make you a fully informed buyer? What was different about your buying process that contributed to your buyer's remorse? Did you buy a bill of goods or a pig in a poke?

2. Think about a couple of intangible things you were recently convinced to "buy" by someone at work. A new job, an idea, a concept, a new hire, a new project, a change in a plan or budget, an investment. One "purchase" that you were totally happy with. Another that caused you in some way to have buyer's remorse. What were the causes of your buyer's remorse? Were you in a hurry and bought before you'd done all your research? Were the products you purchased in each case wants or needs? What was different about your buying process that contributed to your buyer's remorse? Did you buy a bill of goods or a pig in a poke?

3. Think about a couple of intangible things you were recently "sold" by your significant other or children. The need for a new car. New house. New TV, phone, computer, a vacation. Your children being genuinely sorry for something they did wrong and not deserving any sort of punishment. Permission for your children to do something or go somewhere. One intangible you were happy you "bought" and one that you were unhappy that you "bought." What did you do differently in the cases where you were unhappy?

4. Look at your last two months' credit card bills. How many subscriptions are you paying for and how much are you paying per month? They add up quickly. Are you getting your money's worth? If not, why haven't you cancelled them?

5. Have the instances when you experienced buyer's remorse caused you to change your definition of wants and needs? If so, in what ways?

6. Have the instances when you experienced buyer's remorse caused you to make changes to your buying process? If so, what are those changes and have they made you a more astute buyer?

7. Think about a couple of times when you didn't buy something you were being sold that you wished you had. What didn't you buy? What do you wish you had done differently? How do these instances compare to those when you had buyer's remorse?

As you might guess based on the chapters you've read so far, I've been taught many lessons on the importance of being an astute, fully informed buyer. For whatever reason, even when I'm being sold something, I feel as though I need to get a deal done. Wait a minute, I'm not the one selling, I'm buying. Why am I in a hurry? I understand the person doing the selling being in a hurry and needing to get the deal done. But what continues to amaze me is why, when I'm doing the buying not the selling, I'm the one in a hurry. One of the things I've learned about being an astute buyer is that astute buyers don't buy until they know whether what they're being sold is a want or a need, what the seller's motivation is, and whether they are fully informed about the product being sold to them and the person doing the selling.

A prime example of why it's essential for you to understand what is being sold to you and why, and the motivations of the salespeople doing the selling, is my "voluntary" resignation from Cyberonics. Recall from previous chapters that I was asked to resign after false options backdating allegations by SunTrust Capital Markets caused the SEC to request that Cyberonics conduct a complete investigation of every option granted by the company over the previous thirteen years. Because I failed to understand my needs regarding the product I was being sold— resigning my job—and failed to understand what I was being sold and why, and failed to understand the motivations of the sales-persons, namely the Cyberonics board and their legal counsel, I was sold and regrettably bought a "product" that destroyed my career, reputation, and net worth. I allowed myself to be anything but a fully informed buyer.

In any negotiation, both sides are selling and buying. Both sides need to understand their respective needs and whether what they're being sold satisfies those needs. Up until the week before the Cyberonics' board tried to "sell" me on resigning on their terms, I had no idea there was any doubt about my future at Cyberonics. That is, until the Cyberonics board excluded its chairman and CEO, namely me, from a board meeting at which the audit committee's outside counsel was going to present its full options investigation report. When the audit committee's chairman called me on his way to the airport and didn't apol-ogize for excluding me, but simply informed me that the board received the full report and had to adjourn due to travel sched-ules, my confidence became outright panic. Was I about to be fired from Cyberonics or asked to resign? For doing what? I knew I was about to be "sold" something. I just didn't know what and why.

The following week, Cyberonics' outside SEC counsel called my lawyer and told him that the board wanted me to resign. He also told my lawyer that whatever future actions the SEC took against me would depend on whether I cooperated with the board, meaning resigning and agreeing to less than what I was owed under my contract. At this point, instead of panicking and feeling intimidated, I should have stepped back, recognized that it was the board, not me, who was in a rush to get a deal done, and calmly figured out what the board was trying to sell me, or jam down my throat, and why.

Had I done so, I no doubt would have asked myself and eventually the board the following questions to better understand what I was being sold, why I was being sold that product, and the motivations of the salespeople:

1. Why did the company's SEC lawyer call my lawyer and ask me to resign instead of one or more board members meeting with me and asking me to resign, which is standard protocol and professional courtesy?

2. Why did the board deny me all due process including an opportunity to face my "accusers," whomever they were?

3. Why did the board refuse to let me see the options report that was later provided to the SEC and summarized in a press release three days after I resigned?

4. If I had done something wrong and the SEC could legitimately take some sort of action

against me, why was the board asking me to resign instead of terminating me for cause, in which case they would owe me nothing?

5. If I resigned as requested, would Cyberonics and the SEC indemnify me from any further inquiry, investigation, legal or enforcement action so I could get on with my career?

6. The board was putting the bum's rush on me to get a deal done. Why? And was doing a deal quickly in my best interest?

Had I known then what I know now and/or had a confidante who would have given me the advice I'm now offering you, my answers to the above questions would have made me realize that the board and its SEC lawyers were trying to sell me a very expensive "pill" for a terminal illness that didn't exist. An illness on which they had done extensive testing but refused to show me the test results. And a "pill" they knew wasn't a cure but was career, reputation, and financial suicide.

It may be helpful for you to understand why I was such a sucker for an obvious pig in a poke so you can avoid a similar mistake. I was widely known as one of the most passionate CEO's in America. Everyone inside and outside Cyberonics knew I was totally committed to Cyberonics' mission of improving the lives of people touched by treatment-resistant illnesses. Everyone also knew that because of my mother's suicide, I was a zealot when it came to providing people a way out of their severe depression other than suicide. At Cyberonics, starting at the top, we did things the right way because that was the only way to accomplish our mission. I was especially proud of the fact that I created a nonzero-sum game at Cyberonics, meaning that if we improved patients' lives, all employees' personal, professional, and financial dreams would be realized. I led from the front, was the tip of the spear in every fight, and was regarded as being principled to a fault. The integrity of Cyberonics and VNS therapy were of paramount importance to me. I was clearly someone who would do everything for the Cyberonics' mission and people whose lives were touched by medically refractory epilepsy and treatment-resistant depression.

During the six-month options investigation, Cyberonics, VNS therapy, and I were under siege. As chairman and CEO, I was totally emasculated by the media and Wall Street. All the support for FDA approval I had garnered in Washington, that we needed for insurance coverage for VNS for depression, totally disappeared. Cyberonics' stock was being slaughtered. Major insurance companies and Medicare were refusing to extend their favorable coverage policies from epilepsy to depression. When our vice president of human resources and I did extensive analyses that showed there was nothing wrong with Cyberonics' option-granting process and option grants, we were told by SEC counsel that while our analyses were good, the SEC would never accept it. In early November 2006, as the options investigation was coming to an end, I didn't seem to be adding value to Cyberonics or its mission. Unlike in previous difficult situations at Cyberonics, I seemed to be more the problem than the solution. The board not talking to me and treating me like a pariah only made matters worse.

When the Cyberonics board shut me out, I was devastated. All I could think about was the company's mission and my mother. And that the entire universe was telling me I was the one preventing Cyberonics from accomplishing its mission and honoring my promise to my mother. So I did what I perceived to be the right thing, trusted the board and resigned. I thought that if I resigned, Cyberonics would be free to accomplish its mission in depression without me and I would be free to continue my career improving people's lives elsewhere. Think again. Cyberonics and the SEC had other plans.

Three days after my resignation, Cyberonics issued a press release announcing my resignation and the results of the options investigation. Anyone reading that press release knew I was a fighter who was totally committed to Cyberonics' mission and would resign only if I did something very wrong. Yet the press release, much to my and seemingly everyone else's shock, said there were no backdated options, only accounting errors associated with option measurement dates that necessitated non-cash charges that had no effect on Cyberonics' past or future operations. By deceiving me into resigning before I saw the options report and not allowing me to explain the reasons for my resignation to anyone inside or outside Cyberonics, the board made sure the reasons for my resignation were left up to the vivid imaginations of the media, Wall Street, the FDA, employees, potential employers. Even though the SEC's inquiry and Cyberonics' options investigation were over within three months of my resignation, my right to free speech to set the record straight regarding my resignation wasn't returned until I received a closure letter from the SEC four and a half years later. By then, my career and reputation had long since been buried.

The board did a great job selling me on something they knew wasn't in my best interests because they knew that my needs were to honor my mother and do the right thing for patients. Too bad I didn't understand the sellers' wants, needs, and motivations as well as they understood mine. I paid a huge price for the board's and the SEC's bill of goods. The only value I received are these lessons regarding being an astute buyer, which I am now grateful to share with you:

1. Only trust a salesperson who will show you
    what's in the bag before you buy it. Meaning
    only trust a salesperson who seems committed
    to helping you become a fully informed buyer.

2. Never buy anything until you know the seller's
    motivations and what's in it for the seller.

3. Buy only once you completely understand your
    wants and needs and which of your wants and
    needs that product will satisfy.

4. Never be in a rush to do the seller's job, which
    is to close a deal quickly. Make the seller
    answer all your questions and take your time.
    There's always another house, another car,
    another deal that might be better for you.

If ever there was a true test of how astute a buyer each of us is, it's car buying. The car companies have convinced us through their ubiquitous, very effective advertising that when we buy a car, we're not just buying transportation, we're buying an identity, status, a lifestyle, and lifelong happiness (at least until it's time to buy the next new car). Think about the last time you bought a car. Did you know exactly what you were looking for? Did you know your needs and wants? Did you have a budget? Did the salesperson listen to your needs and wants, and was he or she committed to making you a fully informed buyer? Did the salesperson answer or dodge your questions? Did the salesperson admit when they didn't know the answer to your questions, then immediately go get that answer? Did the salesperson sell you what you were looking for or the car that he or she needed you to buy? The process you used to buy your most recent car is likely a good indication of the process you use to buy most things. Does that process suggest that you are an astute buyer?

I recently helped a friend buy a new car. After I asked her a series of questions, she and I knew exactly what she was looking for, which was the best lease deal with a certain amount down and thirty-six monthly payments on a small to midsize SUV. Note that we were first and foremost looking for the *best lease deal* on a certain category of car, instead of a *car*. After doing online research and reading reviews, we narrowed her choice down to Acura, Ford, Range Rover, and Toyota/Lexus.

We then went to those dealerships, met a salesperson, told him or her exactly what we were looking for and started the process. Once my friend narrowed her choices down by looking at, sitting in, and test-driving each SUV, it was time to determine if the salesperson understood that she was looking for a lease deal on a car, not a car. I would tell the salesperson that I had leased a lot of cars and in order for us to make a fully informed decision on a thirty-six-month lease with a certain amount down, we needed to know the net price of the car after all discounts and rebates (the financed amount), the end of lease residual value expressed as a percentage of the net financed price, the annual interest rate used to determine the monthly payment, and the monthly payment. As regards on leases, car dealerships like to confuse customers by quoting a "money factor," such as 0.000025, which appears to be a really low interest rate. The reality is that you have to multiply the "money factor" by 2,400 to get the annual interest rate, which on a money factor of 0.000025 would be 6%, definitely not a good deal. I also mentioned to the salesperson that we specifically wanted the annual interest rate, *not* the money factor.

All the salespeople then went to their sales manager and finance manager to get their "best deal." Only one, the Range Rover salesman, came back not only with all the information we requested, but he also came back with the finance manager to answer all of our questions. Obviously they understood our needs and were committed to us making a fully informed decision. The lease deal my friend was being offered by Range Rover was the best but not quite as good a deal as the one advertised on their website. When she pulled up the website and asked why she wasn't getting the same deal, the salesman explained that the online lease deals were for specific cars that were less popular. The finance manager then asked my friend if she would do the deal if they matched the special website lease deal. She said yes, after which the finance manager provided her with the new, better numbers and within thirty minutes the deal was done. Fully informed astute buyers, salespeople committed to creating fully informed buyers, and straightforward sales processes do indeed make sales happen and both buyers and sellers happy.

In many personal interactions, aren't we and those with whom we're interacting selling something? Even if it's just ourselves? Or being sold something? Such as some sort of relationship with the other person? After being married for twenty-one years, the strangest selling and buying situation in which I found myself was dating, specifically online dating. In online dating, you're both the salesperson/seller and the customer/buyer. Depending on which dating site you're on, you get anywhere between thirty and a couple hundred words and five to twenty photos to describe yourself, which is the product you're selling. Likewise for those trying to sell themselves to you. Of course everyone wants to be liked, so people take liberties with their product descriptions and photos. Some people lie about their height and weight. Some post only photos of their faces. Some post only professional photos that have obviously been Photoshopped. Some post photos that are ten years and thirty pounds out of date. Some post photos with friends who are more attractive than them. If the product you're selling is you and the object is to create customers, why in the world would you would sell a product that doesn't exist, when the real you is immediately out of the bag as soon as you meet your date? In other words, if you're selling a Ford, why would you post photos of and describe a BMW in your profile?

One of the many things I found a bit unsettling about online dating is that there are no reviews on the prospective date (product) being sold to you, unlike cars, restaurants, hotels, airlines, clothing, spas, and most other products and services. All you need for most online dating sites is a Facebook account and/or a mobile phone. Since neither Facebook nor the online dating sites are verifying anyone's information, all the information you're seeing online could be a lie.

When I figured this out,, I started using one of several online background check sites to become a better-informed "buyer," especially before I went to a date's home to pick her up or she knew where I lived or was allowed in my home. The first person's background I checked was my own to see what information was available. I was absolutely stunned. Full name. Names of all relatives. Home address. Where I worked. Marital status. Children's and spouse's/former spouse's names and addresses. Houses I owned and what I paid for them. Criminal record if any (I have none). All social media. Bankruptcy/ foreclosure history (I have none). On and on. Everything that I would only want a select few people that I absolutely trust to know about me. Once I discovered that all of this information was available to anyone who had my full name, age, city in which I live, email and/or phone number, I became much more selective about who I gave that info to as part of my online dating "sales" process.

I was equally stunned by what I discovered when I did background checks on prospective dates. Most were exactly what they represented online. However, I did discover prostitutes, convicted drug dealers, women with multiple real estate foreclosures and recent bankruptcies, women with convicted felon ex-husbands, women who were still married and living with their husband, women with multiple recent DUIs, etc. Certainly not the women as described in their online profiles nor the type of woman I would want knowing much, if anything, about me. Consistent with what I learned in the venture capital business, doing your due diligence doesn't guarantee a good investment but it can certainly prevent you from making a bad decision regarding a product you're being sold, whether it be an investment or a date.

Now that I've shared a few lessons regarding the importance of being an astute, fully informed buyer, think about the last time you were being sold something and were really impressed by the salesperson and process. Tangible and intangible "products." Personally and professionally. How about the last sales process and person that you thought were really bad. What distinguished the good sales processes from the bad? The effective salesperson from the ineffective? Think back to major purchases you were happy you made. Didn't you first "buy" the salesperson, then the product they were selling? Once you have the answers to those questions, you will no doubt have a better idea as to what you need to do to be a great salesperson. Regardless of the "product" you're selling.

So let's switch gears and talk about how to be a great salesperson. Think about several recent situations in which you were selling yourself, intangible products or tangible products, personally or professionally. When you're selling:

1. Do you understand the buyer's wants and needs?

2. Are you committed to helping the buyer become fully informed?

3. Do you answer the buyer's questions truthfully, including by admitting that you don't know the answer when appropriate?

4. Were you accurately representing or misrepresenting the product? Meaning are you selling a pig in a poke or a bill of goods by either misrepresenting the product, dodging the buyer's questions, or purposely not disclosing important aspects about the product to the buyer?

5. What sales tools do you use? Do you use your customer as a sales tool?

6. What percentage of your "customers" are repeat customers?

7. Why do certain customers only "buy" from you once or twice?

8. On a scale of one to five, five being the best, how effective a salesperson are you at work, meaning professionally, and outside of work, meaning personally? Make a list of the things you need to do in each case to be better.

Are you a salesperson at work? Even if you don't work in sales, aren't you always selling something at work? Yourself, your ideas, your department to other departments in the company. The company and its products to everyone you talk to outside the company. The company to prospective employees. Your accomplishments and achievements to receive a bonus or promotion.

As chairman and CEO of Cyberonics, when people would ask me what I did, I'd say that I was in sales. Which was completely true. I was constantly selling. I sold Cyberonics stock and bonds to investors. Career opportunities to people I was interviewing. The viability of our business plans and achievability of our goals to employees and board members. That seemingly impossible challenges could be overcome to employees, board members, investors, etc. Science and data to doctors. Economics to payers and hospitals. Study results, statistics, and data to the FDA. The value of our therapy to patients and their families.

The sales challenge at Cyberonics was beyond daunting. Our mission was to improve the lives of people touched by medically refractory epilepsy and other treatment-resistant disorders. To accomplish that mission, we had to create awareness, acceptance, and demand and sell new medical science and a revolutionary device-based therapy to nine different customer groups accustomed to only using drugs to treat epilepsy. Neurologists, psychiatrists, surgeons, nurses, hospitals, insurance companies, the FDA, patients and their families, and patient advocacy groups. Our challenge was further complicated by the fact that none of our customers directly involved in the purchase decision had ever used an implantable device to treat any of the disorders our device treated and no device company had ever attempted to do what we were doing. The markets we were focused on were drug markets. Our challenge was to convince doctors, hospitals, insurance companies, and patients to use an implantable pacemaker-like device instead of a drug.

As recommended in previous chapters, we created a plan consisting of a series of small doable steps including:

1. Define what product we were selling.

2. Identify each customer group and their needs.

3. Develop a summary of the features, functions, and benefits that we would sell to each customer group.

4. Create and hire the organization to create awareness, acceptance, and demand within each customer group.

5. Develop sales strategies and tactics to effectively create awareness, acceptance, and demand within each customer group.

6. Develop and use all available sales and marketing resources inside and outside the company.

7. Create a sales funnel to measure our performance through a six-step process, starting with patient identification.

The first step in our sales process was to make customers in each of the nine customer groups aware of the revolutionary new science we pioneered regarding the vagus nerve and our revolutionary implantable device-based therapy. Second we had to convince those customers to accept the new science as valid and our device-based therapy as safe and effective. Last, we had to create demand for our device and successfully sell it to customers who were aware of and accepted our science. Given that we were a relatively small company compared to behemoths such as Medtronic, we knew we had to create and use sales and marketing resources outside the company.

Which type of customers do you think are the best customers? Fully informed customers or customers who only know the positives and ways in which your product beats the competition? Because we were selling revolutionary new science and a revolutionary new device-based therapy, we believed that our company, science, therapy, and every Cyberonics employee had to be viewed as credible by all our customers. We also knew that positive customer experiences were also one of the most valuable outside sales tools we had. As a result, we firmly believed in, and implemented, sales and marketing strategies and tactics to create fully informed customers who knew exactly what VNS was and what it wasn't according to all available data. To us, making sure that our customers knew what VNS wasn't was as important as having them know what VNS was to ensure that Cyberonics and VNS delivered on its promises and maximized the number of satisfied customers whose expectations were met.

Remember underpromise and overdeliver from the last chapter? We/I might have failed to effectively manage investors' expectations by underpromising and overdelivering, but we did an outstanding job of managing customers' expectations because we were honest about ("sold") what VNS wasn't. Our track record creating satisfied customers speaks for itself. Our revolutionary device-based therapy outsold implantable cardiac defibrillators, which were a follow-on product for cardiac pacemakers, by more than **two to one** in the first two years after launch and 85% of patients elected to continue with our therapy by having a new generator implanted when their previous generator reached end of battery life/service.

We effectively sold what our product was and wasn't by providing all the data available from all our pre-FDA approval and post-approval studies, and our first-of-its-kind patient registry so that doctors, nurses, patients, and insurance companies could decide whether VNS was right for a specific patient. We provided more data than was available for all the drugs—our competition—combined. As previously mentioned, the registry data showed how patients with certain types of seizures and comorbidities responded to VNS. If those patients didn't respond as well as others, doctors and patients would know that VNS wasn't as effective in those patients. Similarly, we provided data from all the VNS studies and registry that showed that less than 10% of patients treated with VNS became seizure-free. By providing all the data regarding what VNS was, we simultaneously provided the data showing what it wasn't.

Regardless of what you're selling, providing all the data on your product is especially important if your competition doesn't do so. Going back to the online dating example, if you provide your accurate height, weight, marital status, profession, and recent photos, when you meet someone you immediately have credibility for being honest and exactly what you represented. Cyberonics was similar. No drug companies had registries. Why? Because according to neurologists, the effectiveness of drugs declines over time and most drugs have significant side effects that cause patients to switch to another drug. Most drug companies also published only a subset of data from the studies that showed positive results. The data from the negative studies never saw the light of day in the company's literature, peer-reviewed journal articles, or the product's FDA labeling. I still don't understand on what basis the FDA not only condones drug companies' selective disclosure of important data, but also supports such selective disclosure by not requiring *all* relevant data to be in the product labeling—which is controlled by the FDA. I guess for some products and companies, fully informed customers aren't the best customers.

Thinking about your personal and professional selling situations. Have you been able to use highly credible outside sales and marketing resources that your customers view as independent experts? An obvious example is references. Personal or professional references if you're selling yourself. Customer references if you're selling a product. References can be major positives if they're regarded as independent experts. But they can also be negatives if they're viewed as having little relevant knowledge or expertise or certain people are excluded from your reference list.

When I was in the venture capital business, one way we evaluated a member of a management team was the quality of their reference list. Did it include bosses from whatever relevant jobs they had in the past ten years? Did it include peers? Did it include people who reported to them? And did their references have the experience to comment on the person's ability to do the job for which they were being interviewed or had been hired? Note that good reference checkers always go beyond whatever list you provide. Why? Because it's the rare person who can't provide the names of six or seven people that think you walk on water. Both in the venture business and at Cyberonics, when checking references, we would always ask the provided reference, "Who else should I talk to who has a different opinion or perspective than you?"

At Cyberonics, one of the keys to our sales success was that we developed and used outside, independent sales and marketing tools, starting with the FDA. Yes, you read correctly. The FDA. Why and how? Because we provided all of our data in our product labeling approved by the FDA, including the Summary of Safety and Effectiveness that was readily available on their website. Allow me to explain: Three of the features that distinguished VNS from its competition (drugs) and effectively sold VNS were (1) sustained and accumulating safety and effectiveness over time, (2) a growing percentage of patients on VNS that were able reduce the drugs they were taking, and (3) over 80% patient continuation rates. Our product literature, videos, etc., all highlighted these significant differential advantages and when skeptical doctors, insurance companies, or patients wanted proof, we would refer them to the most credible of all outside experts—the FDA's website.

The other highly credible outside experts we cultivated to support our sales and marketing success at Cyberonics were doctors and patients. Doctors who participated in studies, enrolled patients in the registry, treated patients with VNS, did mechanism-of-action research, and then spoke to their colleagues, wrote papers, or spoke at annual industry symposia. These doctors were considered highly credible experts by all of our customers. Once we developed these credible doctor and patient experts, we created as many venues as possible for them to share their experience, including post-approval studies, peer-reviewed literature, physician and patient education events, on our website, in our marketing literature.

So for any of your customers, who and what is the most effective salesperson and sales tool? What I learned at Cyberonics is that the most effective sales tool for any customer is that specific customer's words, actions, and experience. Get someone you're trying to sell to sing your product's praises and they soon become a customer.

Have the lessons I've learned and shared with you convinced you that in order to master you from the inside out you need to become an astute, fully informed buyer and great salesperson who consistently creates fully informed customers? I hope so, because if I knew then what I know now about being an astute buyer and great salesperson in every personal and professional situation in which I was selling or being sold something, my family and I would have considerably more abundance on every level. And our collective net worth would be over twenty times what it is today.

CHAPTER 14

THE WHITE FLAG VICTORY RULE

"The law of diminishing returns means that even the most beneficial principle will become harmful if carried far enough." — Thomas Sowell, economist and author, Rose and Milton Friedman Senior Fellow, Hoover Institution, Stanford University

---

THE LAW OF DIMINISHING **returns describes the point at which the profits or benefits gained are less than the amount of money or energy invested. Said another way, the point at which the gain isn't worth more pain.** Diminishing returns will eventually become negative returns if we keep doing what produced the diminishing returns.

The *Mastering You from the Inside Out* white flag victory rule states that one should stop, let go of, walk away from, and/or sell whatever it is we're doing, thinking, or holding on to once we've reached the point of diminishing, or in some cases negative, returns. And although we may feel as though we're hoisting the white flag and surrendering, declare victory instead—victory over diminishing and negative returns, no gain, more pain, and doing damage to that which is of value to us.

Think of a professional athlete who played way too long, way past their prime, as a mere shadow of their previous Hall of Fame self? Who didn't know when to walk away. Who looked strange in their new team's uniform. How about Peyton Manning in a Broncos uniform? Brett Favre in a New York Jets and Minnesota Vikings uniform? Jerry Rice in a Raiders and Seattle Seahawks uniform? Joe Montana in a Kansas City Chiefs uniform? How did you feel watching them in their twilight years? Uncomfortable? Sad? Embarrassed for them? Even though they were still being paid millions of dollars?

Now think about times when you "played" too long, past your "prime," meaning past the point of diminishing returns. Perhaps past the point where you were doing damage to or destroying something that was of great value to you. "Played" meaning continued a debate or argument; held on to an investment, house, or car; stayed in a career or job too long; or continued to do the same things over and over expecting different results (one definition of insanity). Let's explore your answers to three questions:

Question 1: Can you think of a job or career in which you stayed too long? Past the point of the emotional, intellectual and/or financial rewards? Perhaps after which you had opportunities to change jobs or careers. Are you in such a job or career now? What diminishing or negative emotional, intellectual, or financial returns did you experience or are you experiencing? What did you learn from or are you doing to change the trajectory of your returns on your significant investment of time and energy? What negative effects did your diminishing returns have on your health? On your relationships with your significant other, your children, your friends? On your career, job prospects, and earning potential going forward?

During my time in the venture capital business, I observed many entrepreneurs who viewed the companies they founded as their babies they never wanted to let go of. If those entre-preneurs were the founders and CEOs of a start-up, often those start-ups—privately held "babies"—grew rapidly into venture capital-backed teenagers, young adults, and publicly traded mature companies generating hundreds of millions dollars. Many of these successful companies outgrew the founder's experience and would have performed better with a CEO with different experience and skills. For founders of companies and entrepreneurs, it's very important to know when to let go, meaning step aside in favor of a more experienced CEO, or sell the company. It all depends on when the point of diminishing returns is reached.

One or more of the following would occur when a company outgrew the founder and CEO's experience. If the founder's, investors' and board's intentions were to sell the company sooner rather than later, then the founder would stay as CEO and the company would be sold prior to the company outgrowing the founder's experience and skills. Of course, the question always was, "Did we sell too soon?"

If all parties agreed that the founder's limited experience was holding back his or her "baby," he or she would step aside into another role in the company, such as chairman or vice president, and help the board find the most qualified CEO. In this case, the founder would still get all the credit for founding the company and his or her stock would, in most cases, be worth considerably more than if he or she had stayed in the CEO role. This is exactly what happened at Cyberonics, when the founder, an engineer and former vice president of business development, moved from CEO first to vice president of engineering then to chairman of the board then to board member. Had the founder stayed as CEO, his stock would have been worth very little. Under my leadership, his stock was worth over $20 million.

In the third scenario, the founder and CEO disagrees with the investors and the board and absolutely refuses to step aside and hire someone more qualified. The founder is often then fired by the board and is no longer associated with the company. In this case, the founder ends up owning less stock than he or she would have otherwise owned and that stock ends up being worth much less than it would have otherwise been worth.

In the last scenario, a strong visionary founder remains CEO with the help of a strong board and creates an extraordinarily successful company. There are many examples, including Bill Gates at Microsoft, Steve Jobs at Apple, Mark Zuckerberg at Facebook, Richard Branson at Virgin.

Like many entrepreneurs whose companies' needs outgrew their experience, at Cyberonics I learned a very expensive lesson regarding the importance of following the white flag victory rule before the point of diminishing—or, in my case, disastrous returns. When we received the FDA's approval to use VNS for treatment-resistant depression, Cyberonics and I had just accomplished what most believed to be totally impossible. Not only did we overturn a not-approvable decision in record time, but we also had the opportunity to improve millions of lives.

Cyberonics at the time was generating more than $100 million in sales from the epilepsy market alone, eight years after FDA approval. Ten times as many Americans suffered from treatment-resistant depression than medically refractory epilepsy. Meaning that with FDA approval, in several years Cyberonics' annual revenue could have potentially exceeded $1 billion!

In 2005, after we received approval to use VNS for depression, Cyberonics' stock price gave the company a total market value of over $1 billion, more than forty times its value ten years earlier when I became CEO. My fully vested, fully tradable shares that represented only 50% of my total stock were worth over $30 million. All I had to do to sell those shares was to dial ten numbers on my mobile phone and instruct my broker to sell. That over $30 million or proceeds would have generated over $1.3 million in tax-free income per year!

In July 2005, it seemed Cyberonics and I had very bright futures ahead of us. There didn't seem to be a challenge we couldn't overcome. And the upcoming challenge of extending insurance coverage from epilepsy to depression seemed straightforward.

Unfortunately, what I failed to recognize was that I had made so many powerful powers that be enemies in overcoming past challenges, there was no way I could accomplish Cyberonics' mission or manifest my personal, professional, and financial intentions at the company going forward. My enemies were simply too powerful and too determined to destroy me and VNS. With twenty-twenty hindsight, it's obvious that I had become as much, if not more, of a liability than an asset.

Had I known in July 2005 what I know now, or had an experienced confidante who was advising me, I would have implemented the white flag victory rule, resigned, left the "game" in my "prime," and eliminated my enemies' need to destroy me and, even more important, destroy the only FDA-approved treatment for severe treatment-resistant depression. By resigning, I would have given my enemies what they wanted. Namely that Cyberonics' chairman and CEO and "status quo disruptor and shit disturber in chief" would have shut his big mouth and disappeared. Had I done so, I would have perhaps left Cyberonics and VNS for TRD with an opportunity to improve the lives of millions of Americans like my mother. I would have also left with my share of the value I created, my reputation as a neuroscience industry pioneer intact, and no doubt had many other opportunities to create personal, professional, and financial abundance.

Instead, I gave my enemies no choice but to destroy me

and VNS for depression on their terms only one year later. And those terms weren't pretty. Although VNS for depression was FDA approved, it was totally discredited to the point where no insurance company would cover it, thereby denying depression patients the same access to the therapy enjoyed by epilepsy patients. My fate wasn't much better. Although I was never officially charged with any wrongdoing, my career, reputation, and net worth were destroyed by my forced resignation without any due process under pressure from the SEC. Not only did the SEC force my resignation under a cloud of suspicion, but it also made sure that my career and reputation were dead and buried by making me wait four years after the Cyberonics' inquiry was over to send me a closure letter and give me back my rights to free speech and my right to publicly defend myself. Unfortunately none of the net worth, reputation, or career I lost were included in that closure letter.

All things considered, the lesson I learned at Cyberonics regarding "playing" past my "prime" was a very expensive lesson. For a lot of people. Like a big rock dropping into a lake, the ripple effects went on and on. The only FDA-approved treatment for millions of Americans with treatment-resistant depression was destroyed. My opportunity to improve the lives of millions of people touched by treatment-resistant epilepsy, depression, and other illnesses was taken away from me. My opportunity to honor my commitment to my mother was destroyed. My career, reputation, net worth, and opportunity to earn a living doing what I was most qualified to do was destroyed. Irreparable damage was done to my then marriage with the mother of my children. My health deteriorated. I gained thirty-five pounds. I had no self-esteem. For years I was like a zombie in the land of the walking dead and not the husband or father I once was. At least I learned a very important lesson that I can now share with you to help you and master you from the inside out and implement the white flag victory rule when appropriate.

Question 2: Do you suffer from last-word-itis when it comes to debates or arguments at work and at home? Do you at times continue to debate and argue about something when there's no chance of winning the debate or agreeing on whatever it is you're arguing about? Is there one thing that you and your significant other have repeatedly debated or argued about without any resolution? Money, children, sex, politics? If so, what damage has your repeated arguing about the same thing done to your relationship? And to your work performance and other personal and professional relationships? To your and your significant other's health?

Whenever I observed professionals like me not knowing when it was time to let go, it seemed as though their reticence was directly correlated to how personal the situation was for them. Can anything be more personal than your relationship with your spouse or significant other? In thirty-nine total years of marriage in two marriages I've had my share of disagreements with my spouses. I never learned to disengage from the "discussion" when it became clear that we were past the point of diminishing returns and that more talk would only worsen the situation and provide more fuel for future disagreements on the same topic. Instead of letting go of whatever it was my then-wife and I had disagreed about in the one, two, three, five, or ten previous debates on the same subject, one or both of us continued the disagreement and seemed to always be prepared to re-engage in the same argument.

Just like driving a car, managing relationships by constantly looking in the rearview mirror instead of where you're going is not a good idea. Unless you think crashing your car or having your marriage end in divorce, which mine unfortunately did, are good ideas. My recommendation is to concede the last word victory to your significant other, let go of whatever it was you were arguing about once and for all, apologize for continuing the argument, and do something to bring you both back into the present. Go for a walk holding hands, hug and kiss, eye gaze, and breath and sound together. Whatever you need to do to bring all your senses, your heart, and mind into the present and out of the past.

There's nothing like emails, texts, Facebook messages, and other forms of electronic communication to prolong last-word-itis, debates, and arguments well past the point of diminishing returns. The white flag victory rule really applies to these forms of communication. Think about several recent emails and texts you wish you'd never sent. What do you wish you had done differently? Before sending any such text or email, did you:

- Know what you'd hoped to accomplish with the text or email?
- Did you carefully consider the likely impact your text or email would have on its recipient and the impact the recipient's reaction would have on what you hoped to accomplish with the email or text? If the likely impact was best-case neutral and worst-case negative to very negative, why did you send it?
- Did you "sleep on it" for twenty-four hours, then reconsider the previous two questions before you sent the text or email?
- Did you have an unbiased friend or confidante read the proposed text or email, ask you the above questions, and give you their unvarnished feedback?

I have only recently started consciously applying the white flag victory rule to my last-word-itis disorder with great success. I am quickly learning the significant benefits of disengaging from senseless debates and significantly editing, never sending or holding for the appropriate time texts and emails to all those with whom I have important relationships. For me, it's all about letting go of the past and realizing as much pleasure and as little conflict as possible from the present and future.

Question 3: Are there things from the past that that you can't let go of—meaning leave in the past—that are holding you back? Something that was said or done to you when you were young by your parents or siblings? Something that was said or done to you by a spouse or significant other? Something that was said or done to you at work? How about something that was said or done to you and the person who said or did it apologized and you forgave them? Did you still hang on to whatever it was that you forgave even though that same thing wasn't done or said to you again by that same person? Think about the times when this baggage didn't serve you and caused you to do or say things you later regretted? What work have you done to let go of this baggage?

One thing I observed in my study and practice of tantra yoga is that many people, myself included, have great difficulty letting go of all type of baggage from the past. Including both positive and negative energies that keep us from being fully present in the moment. We want to hang on to positive energies, perhaps like the professional athletes who play past their prime, and we can't seem to ever let go of our negative energies baggage. Whenever we hang on to energies, we deprive ourselves of the energies that come to us by being fully present in the moment. If today all we think about is what a perfect day yesterday was, surely we will miss all or part of the pleasure and bliss that's available today. If we are carrying around multiple fears and triggers from the past, aren't we living in the past and ignoring all the experience, knowledge, and wisdom we have acquired since those fears and triggers first arose?

As discussed in Chapter 2, The Origin Challenge, even if we cannot "let go of" issues from our past, at least if we're aware of them, we can minimize their influence on and control of our present. In my case I'm doing a much better job of letting go of or managing my fear of abandonment, disease to please, lack of personal boundaries, inability to pick my battles, reliance on me, myself, and I, and last-word-itis.

How are you at letting go of something that someone said or did for which they apologized and you forgave them? How have others been at letting go of something for which you have apologized and been forgiven? Here's what I know now that I wish I knew then regarding apologies and forgiveness in important relationships. I call it the remorse-apology-forgiveness contract:

- I am not a mind reader, so if something I've said or done has offended or hurt someone, I think it is their responsibility to calmly tell me what I've said or done and how it made them feel. It is then my responsibility to not get defensive and ask whatever questions I need answered to understand what I've done.
- If I understand and feel remorse ("deep regret or guilt for a wrong committed"), it is my responsibility to say I'm sorry or apologize. If I say I'm sorry or apologize, I am committing to try my best to not do or say the same thing again. In other words, leave the behavior or words for which I am sorry in the past. If I'm truly sorry for what I have said or done, not only will I say I'm sorry, but I will also act like I'm sorry by not repeating the offending behavior or words. Actions speak louder than words.
- If the person to whom I have apologized forgives me, they have a responsibility to not bring up my offending or hurtful behavior or words unless I repeat that

behavior or those words. In other words, join me in leaving my "offense" in the past.

- Because nobody is perfect, if I repeat the offensive words or behavior once or twice, I deserve the benefit of the doubt, especially if I catch myself and acknowledge that I made a mistake before having to be reminded of my repeated offensive, hurtful words or behavior. However, if I repeat the offending words or behavior over and over, that's an indication that I felt no true remorse, my apology was inauthentic, I don't really care about the person's feelings, and didn't deserve forgiveness.

- Of course, the same is true if the roles are reversed. Namely that if I was the one offended or hurt, received an apology, and was the one doing the forgiving, but kept bringing up the offensive behavior.

Had my wife of twenty-one years and the mother of my children and I understood, agreed to, and consistently honored what I now call the remorse-apology-forgiveness contract, I'm fairly certain that we would have argued much less, trusted each other more, and would have provided each other with the support we needed to maintain our marriage through its many challenges. If we only knew then what I know now.

There are many techniques that we can use to let go of energies, triggers, and baggage from the past. One technique I learned in tantra is to use breathing and sounding to activate your vagus nerve and move unwanted energies, triggers, and baggage up and out of your body. This can also help you keep unwanted energies, triggers, and baggage from taking over your decision making at critical times. Although there are many different types of "breath work" and breathing and sounding techniques, the basic one is fairly simple, and effective if regularly practiced.

- Inhale deeply through your nose filling your stomach and lungs. Imagine that you're breathing up all the energies, feelings, or thoughts that you would like to get rid of.
- Hold that breath.
- Exhale through your mouth and make whatever sound is consistent with energies, feelings, etc. that you would like to move out, at a volume consistent with the level of those feelings/energies.

As an example, if you're feeling frustrated and you need to make a clearheaded decision about something, breathe that frustration up with a long, slow inhale, then forcibly exhale with a very loud sound of frustration. Repeat for ten to fifteen breaths and feel the difference. You will likely be fully present, free from your frustration and able to make a clear-headed decision.

Breathing and sounding also magnify and move positive energies. Are you and your significant other louder when you are angry at each other or when you're making love? If you are louder when you're angry, the next time you are feeling pleasure, breathe all that pleasure up, then sing it out loudly with a powerful exhale rejoicing in your pleasure and the fact that you are becoming an awakened and empowered master of your energies. When you do, you will share your pleasure and bliss with your significant other and liberate him or her to powerfully summon and share their pleasure with you in a truly synergistic one plus one equals one hundred way.

I recommend practicing breathing and sounding as a technique to control and move your energies, positive and negative,

every day. The more you practice moving energies and stimu-
lating your vagus nerve the more adept you will be at letting go
of whatever from your past is holding you back. And the more
positive energies, pleasure, and bliss you will be able to summon
and share in the present and future on your way to mastering
you from the inside out.

Considering my origin programming, I never imagined that
hoisting the white flag and "surrendering" was one path to victory.
If I only knew then what I know now.

CHAPTER 15

ARE YOU SCALABLE?

Scalability is the capacity to be changed in size, scale, or scope to facilitate profitable growth. How scalable are you?

SCALABLE SYSTEMS, NETWORKS, companies, and organizations take full advantage of opportunities for growth by changing in size, scale, and/or scope while *simultaneously increasing efficiency and profitability.* The same goes for people, including you and me, although our profits may include emotional, intellectual, spiritual, professional and financial gains.

We are all managers and CEOs. Professionally at work and personally outside of work. Even if the only person we manage is ourselves. The more scalable our management capabilities are, the more profitably we grow, the more opportunities we create and take advantage of, and the more abundance we produce and share. Being scalable personally and professionally, emotionally, intellectually, spiritually, physically, and financially is a key ingredient to mastering you from the inside out. So how scalable are you? Let's find out.

1. Do you have plans for personal or professional growth over the next year or more? If so, your

scalability is important. No one is infinitely elastic emotionally, intellectually, energetically, or financially.

2. Have you assessed your strengths, weaknesses, and resources, including scalability in terms of your plans? If so, you may understand scalability and your need for scalability.

3. Do you know what additional resources you need to implement your growth plan? If so, you may be scalable.

4. When you deploy additional resources to implement your plans, are they proven resources who've been there, done that in terms of what you need them to do for you? Are they experts who are as—if not more—qualified for their jobs as you are for yours? Or do you hire friends or inexpensive, inexperienced people who are less qualified? If you're employing and deploying underqualified people or unproven resources who you need to micromanage, you're probably not scalable.

5. Is your management style one of delegation of responsibility and authority or only partial delegation? If you don't delegate responsibility and authority, you're probably not maximizing your return on the additional people and resources you've employed and deployed. Meaning you're not as scalable as you could and should be.

6. Do you effectively manage the people working for you personally? Housekeepers, real estate

agents, lawyers, therapists, personal trainers, etc. Do you explain exactly what you expect them to do? And then delegate to them the entire job? Or do you delegate only half the job and do the other half yourself? Do you hold them accountable for doing the job as you've defined it? What do you do if they aren't doing the job correctly? Do the job for them? Or manage them by explaining what they are doing incorrectly, holding them accountable to improve, and if necessary replacing them? If (1) you didn't delegate the entire job to them, (2) you're accommodating and indulging their nonperformance and not managing them, or (3) you're doing their job for them, then you're probably not scalable.

7. Think about the people working for you whom you've had to let go or replace. Was the problem them or you? Meaning did you fail to hire the right person or effectively manage them? If so, perhaps the issue was you and your management skills not being scalable.

8. Are you comfortable asking the people working for you to do specific things within a specific time frame? How about providing those working for you with feedback on what they're doing well and what they could be doing better? If you're not comfortable doing these things, you're probably not scalable.

9. How frequently do you ask for feedback from important people at work and outside of work?

Including your partners, boss, those above you at work, and your significant other at home. Especially feedback on what you could do better or what you need to do to be promoted, get a raise, etc. If you're not regularly asking for feedback from those who control your destiny and scalability at work and at home, you're probably not scalable.

10. Are you a procrastinator who always seems to be overloaded and behind? If so, you're probably not scalable.

11. Do you spend a lot of time talking about how busy you are? If so, you're probably not scalable.

12. Are you a sole proprietor with a management problem? If so you're probably not scalable.

The tragedies, traumas, successes, mistakes and failures I've shared in this book have taught that in order to be scalable—in order to grow while also increasing efficiency and profitability—each of us needs to (1) have a personal and professional growth plan, (2) accurately assess our individual strengths and weaknesses, including scalability, relative to that plan, (3) hire, employ, and deploy the people and resources to complement our strengths and weaknesses, (4) delegate responsibility *and* authority, (5) effectively manage ourselves and the people and resources on our team, and (6) regularly communicate. The purpose of all those scalability building blocks being to expand and grow while simultaneously increasing efficiency and profitability!

Writing this book to build a new brand and business as a personal and professional development speaker, teacher, and confidante is a testament to the importance of personal scalability. For the past four years, several people familiar with my story have suggested that I write a book. One of those people was a university professor who wrote and had a book published by one of the major publishing houses ten years ago. Although her book was neither a commercial success nor a launch pad for a new brand or business, I took her advice and she helped me write in-depth chapter summaries for my proposed book. Without first assessing my emotional, intellectual, energetic, and experiential scalability. And without identifying my target audience, my goals for the book, my competition, or the current market for memoir, the type of book I initially planned to write. Those chapter summaries were sent to her publisher and predictably, given what I know now, rejected. The message? I wasn't scalable when it came to writing a successful book. I didn't have a plan, I hadn't accurately assessed my strengths and weaknesses, and I hadn't hired and deployed the resources to complement my strengths and weaknesses.

After moving to Southern California in late 2017, I met several other published authors, who encouraged me to learn more about the book business by going to the La Jolla Writers Conference, widely considered to be one of the best in the country. I took their advice and after day one of the conference, my head was spinning. I not only knew nothing about how to write a successful book, but I also had no clue—and I mean no clue—about how to successfully package, publish, and market a book to facilitate commercial success with a new or existing brand and business.

The speakers and attendees at the conference were speaking the same language as me, namely English, but we were not using the same vocabulary nor did we have common experience. Not even close. I felt like I was back in organic chemistry at Dartmouth when I had no clue what the professor was talking about.

It didn't take long for me to realize that although I may be an expert when it came to commercializing a new medical science, product, and company, I had no plan, knew nothing about, and had neither the people nor the resources to commercialize a new book, brand, and business. Thanks to the conference, my personal scalability improved dramatically because at least I knew what I didn't know, knew my strengths and weaknesses, and knew I needed to hire a been there, done that book/business consultant to help me develop and implement a plan; successfully write, package, publish, and market a book; and develop and commercialize a new personal and professional brand and business in conjunction with the book to accomplish my mission to improve people's lives while at the same time realizing my fair share of the value I have added and will add to the universe. Thanks, Jared, for the lesson on scalability!

Planning is the first building block of personal and professional scalability. Without a plan, we have no clue where we want to go or what we need to do to get there. No context in which to accurately assess our strengths and weakness, including scalability. And no idea of what additional resources we need to profitably grow. When it comes to major personal life changes that are common in today's world, we definitely need a plan and an accurate assessment of our emotional and energetic scalability. Life changes like moving in with your significant other, marriage, having kids, getting involved with someone who has children living at home from a previous marriage, divorce, etc.

Think about the major life changes that have occurred in your life and the lives of your friends that haven't gone well. Like my initial decision to write a book. How many of those changes didn't go well because of scalability issues, namely the people involved didn't have a plan, didn't accurately assess their strengths and weaknesses, and had no clue what resources they needed to grow through those changes? If two people are accustomed to living alone and doing what they want whenever they want, living together is going to require an agreed-upon plan and the emotional scalability to share essentially everything and compromise. Similarly, if two people who are madly in love, and accustomed to sharing their love and intimacy only with each other, want to have children, they need a plan and the emotional, energetic, and financial scalability to not only be good parents, but also preserve their relationship. I'm sure you know at least one couple's marriage that ended in divorce when their children were young because of the following series of unfortunate events.

- They have kids without doing any relationship or financial planning other than agreeing that Mom will quit her job and take care of the kids
- Two kids are born two years apart. Mom is a devoted mother and the kids are her highest priority.
- Dad is a good father but has to work longer hours to make up for the lost income due to Mom no longer working and the additional expenses of having two kids to take care of. His job becomes his highest priority.
- Both Mom and Dad are emotionally and energetically exhausted and have neither the time nor the energy nor a plan to maintain the intimacy that once characterized their relationship.
- Mom and Dad don't make time for each other, don't go out on dates, and rarely have sex. When they do, it's not satisfying. Dad blames Mom's preoccupation with the kids. Mom blames Dad's preoccupation with work.
- Dad and/or Mom find the validation and intimacy they once had with each other elsewhere. First flirting, then

suggestive messages and conversations, then drinks, then adultery.

- One or both get caught. They try therapy. But too little, too late. Marriage over and family destroyed.
- Why? Because of Dad's and Mom's failure to agree on a plan to have kids while simultaneously maintaing their relationship, failure to accurately assess their strengths and weaknesses, including emotional, energetic, and financial scalability, and failure to deploy the additional resources to successfully grow their family.

Emotional and energetic scalability and accurate assessments thereof are also important professionally when it comes to promotions, transfers, new jobs, and starting a company, especially if your intention is to profitably grow.

Most personal and professional growth plans, whether it be moving in with your significant other, getting married, having kids, getting divorced, moving, going back to school, changing jobs, starting a company, making personal investments, buying a new house, commercializing a new medical science and device, and writing a book all require more resources than just us. And personal growth and professional growth have a funny way of happening simultaneously, further compounding the need for us to be scalable as our families and careers take off.

Hiring, employing, and deploying the "right" people and resources and putting them in a position to succeed is one of the prerequisites for being a scalable CEO of your personal and professional life. Starting with yourself based on an accurate assessment of your strengths and weaknesses. One of my discoveries at Cyberonics was that in order to hire and put people in a position to win, we had to understand what exactly was needed in terms of being successful in a particular job and whether the person being considered for that job had the actual experience and personality traits to be successful. Most importantly, experience pioneering new approaches and new solutions to new problems and situations.

At Cyberonics, we had to pioneer almost everything, including new study designs, a new device, new treatment parameters, a new sales and marketing model to create awareness, acceptance and demand for a device-based therapy among different customer constituencies. We needed entrepreneurs who were willing to take risks and try new things. Whether someone thrived in a rapidly changing company and market was more important than whether someone worked at a successful device company or drug company. We hired several very experienced vice presidents from major device and drug companies who had played major roles in launching, marketing, getting approval for, and selling major devices or drugs, including drugs for the treatment of epilepsy or depression. The problem was that we were an early stage, high-growth company that had a device-based alternative to drugs that was neither a drug nor a device but a hybrid of the two. You know the old adage about old dogs learning new tricks? If you had a successful management career at a major drug or device company, of course you *knew* and firmly believed in that company's way of doing things. Your embracing and implementing of that approach is what made you successful. Like many "old dogs," several of the people we hired from drug and device companies couldn't and wouldn't learn Cyberonics' "new tricks." We simply hired the wrong people because we didn't take the time to carefully determine whether the highly credentialed people with great résumés we hired were good fits. Learning as we went, our hiring process and organization became more scalable over time.

The scalability of the promotion process is equally important as the scalability of the hiring process. A lack of scalability is often illuminated when individual contributors are promoted to leadership positions and become ineffective managers. Managing others is a lot more difficult than managing only yourself as an individual contributor. Don't management jobs require much different skill sets as compared to jobs in which we are only managing ourselves? Including hiring the right people, putting people in positions to win, convincing people to listen to you, follow you, do what you need them to do. What do you do to get the people who you were assigned to manage to buy in?

Think about the last people you hired or promoted. To whom did you sell that hire or promotion? Your boss, your peers, your investors, your significant other (in the case of a real estate agent, a family lawyer, etc.)? If you hired or promoted someone, you obviously thought they would do a good job and you convinced others of that fact. If the person you hired or promoted didn't perform, whose credibility was on the line? Yours, because you sold that hire or promotion to others and you, in essence, "promised" to effectively manage that person. Damaged credibility doesn't enhance your scalability.

Are the people you've hired and promoted in the past as qualified for their new jobs as you are for your job? Another of the lessons I learned in the venture capital business and while a CEO is that managers, especially inexperienced managers, often hire people who are less qualified for their jobs than the manager doing the hiring is qualified for theirs. In doing so, the hiring/promoting manager thinks they are hiring/promoting someone who poses no threat to them. In actuality, the reverse is true. If you hire people to work for you who are more qualified for their jobs than you are for yours, they will more than likely be outstanding performers who make you look like a hero. If you hire people who are underqualified for their jobs, they may not threaten you by being someone who might take your job, but they certainly threaten your job because of their likely underperformance.

Think about your best hires or promotions. Are they the people that need micromanagement and to be told what to do or are they the ones who know what to do, come to you with a plan for your input and approval, and then implement their plan with minimal management from you? Are they the ones who will accept minimal delegation or expect you to delegate responsibility and authority? For me, my best hires and promotions were those that expected and deserved delegation, told me what they were going to do, and created a plan that was better than the one I would have created on my own.

Delegation is the third building block of scalability. Delegation is absolutely essential in order for you to maximize your return on the additional people and resources you employ and deploy to implement your plans. In order to put all those who we are managing personally and professionally, including ourselves, in positions to succeed, we need to effectively delegate both responsibility and authority. Profitable scalability is a function of delegation.

Planning is one way to delegate. Plans define goals and allocate resources. Plans determine what additional resources need to be employed and deployed. Once a plan is approved, you and everyone working for you personally and professionally has clearly defined responsibility and authority, knows what goals they are accountable for achieving, and what resources they have available to accomplish their goals. In essence, the plan delegates responsibility and authority to expend the resources and implement each person's and department's portions of the plan. Quarterly review meetings make management of the delegated responsibility and authority straightforward.

At Cyberonics, we repeatedly accomplished what most thought was impossible through thorough planning and delegation of responsibility and authority. Annual planning and budgeting meetings were typically two to three day offsite affairs involving senior management, including the CEO (me), all the vice presidents, and the directors in each department who reported to each of the vice presidents. Each of us would check our titles at the door before every meeting and come together as equals. Each attendee was expected to provide input for the corporate and departmental plans and budgets based on that person's unique experience and knowledge. Every aspect of our business and organization was discussed, sometimes with great passion. Almost everyone in these meetings was an active participant. Why? Because everyone knew that Cyberonics' plans delegated responsibility and authority and that with responsibility and authority came accountability.

Our offsite planning meetings also involved several fun team-building activities to avoid the all-work and no-play syndrome. Given that the senior management team at Cyberonics was a rather competitive bunch, the joke about our team-building activities was that liability waivers, helmets, and/or other forms of protective gear and first aid were often required. I distinctly remember an ATV "tour" near Scottsdale when the tour leader, who looked like he'd been in the desert for a week without a shower and shave, instructed us to ride in single file at a safe distance behind each other because at certain points the trail would abruptly become so narrow that only one ATV at a time could get through. As he approached the first such narrow point, he stopped and turned around to make sure we were following his instructions. Apparently we forgot the instructions because what he saw was six of us at full throttle, racing abreast to be the first one through the hole. The way he shook his head then left us in a cloud of dust suggested that from that point forward, his attitude about our tour was one of "hear no evil, see no evil, and speak no evil." Given that there was a river crossing on the tour, we all came back covered with mud, dirt, and cactus scratches. Ready for the next planning session!

The end result of these offsite planning meetings would be a consensus on an outline of the corporate and each department's plans, goals, and budgets. Using that outline as a guide, each department would then develop detailed plans that would be finalized at another group meeting a couple weeks later. Once the plan was approved, thereby delegating responsibility and authority, every manager at Cyberonics was empowered to do their job as part of the plan. Only exceptions to the plan required any further approval. At the end of every quarter, we would hold review meetings. Bonuses were tied to exceeding the corporate and each department's plans.

Incomplete delegation reduces your scalability. I'm not the greatest delegator when it comes to people I have hired to work for me or my family. A great example is real estate agents who are representing me as a listing agent selling my house or as a buyer's agent helping me buy a house. Instead of delegating the responsibility, authority, and accountability to the listing agent for producing all the sales and marketing materials, I often do it myself. I do the same for both listing and buyer's agents when I create a detailed analysis of recently sold and for-sale comparable homes in the format I prefer. Why do I do the agents' work for them when I am directly or indirectly paying them a 3% commission worth, in most cases, more than $20,000 is beyond me. My time could no doubt be used more profitably elsewhere, meaning I would be more scalable if I effectively managed and delegated.

The fourth building block of personal scalability is effective management. Of ourselves and the other people and resources we've employed and deployed to implement our growth plans. Once you've hired, employed, and deployed the "right" people and resources, and delegated responsibility and authority, your scalability is then a function of how effectively you manage them to do what they've been employed and deployed to do.

One of the secrets to my and the sales force's scalability at Cyberonics was the use of a small chartered jet that enabled me to spend two days in every US sales territory every six months, visiting with doctors, nurses, patients, and their families. These trips improved scalability while simultaneously improving efficiency and profitability. During each five-day week traveling with the sales force, I would visit an average of twenty-five different cities and towns and meet hundreds of neurologists, nurses, and patients in doctors' offices, at physician dinners, and at patient education events. None of our customers and potential customers I met had ever met the CEO of any of our "competitors," let alone had a CEO come to their office or present at a local physician dinner or patient education event. I would ask every person I met what they thought of our product and people, and what Cyberonics should be doing more of or less of to improve more people's lives. I also gave each person I met my card with my mobile phone number and invited them to call me anytime they had any suggestions they wanted to share. The "airfare" for each of these weeks averaged $25,000, which was paid for by the gross profit on the sales of only three vagus nerve stimulators. There was no doubt among anyone at Cyberonics that the effective management of this important resource improved our scalability and profitability.

Managing resources and other people to do things the way you want or the way your growth plan needs is often much more difficult than doing those things yourself. Not just at work but also at home. Let's say you've hired a housekeeper so you can spend more time at work and with your family, but that housekeeper isn't doing something you've asked them to do the way you've asked them to do it. Do you manage them by telling and showing them what they aren't doing correctly or do you just do that task yourself? If you're doing the task yourself, your're sacrificing your scalability by paying the housekeeper the planned amount and receiving less of the planned benefit. All because you're uncomfortable managing the people and resources you employed and deployed? Sounds like a scalability problem. Same goes for jobs assigned to your kids so you can spend more time with your spouse. Like post-dinner clean up. If they don't do the job correctly, do you accommodate and indulge them by doing it for them, thereby sacrificing your relationship scalability?

Doing tasks that you've delegated to others and accommodating and indulging poor performance or nonperformance also sacrifices scalability at work. Whenever you're in a management, leadership, or coaching position, your performance equals the performance of the people you're managing, leading, and coaching. Their performance is your performance. Their scalability is your scalability. Your scalability is the company's scalability. When a manager reports on or complains about the nonperformance of one or more people reporting to them, they are in essence reporting on/complaining about their own nonperformance. At Cyberonics during quarterly review meetings, sales managers would often say, "My region missed its numbers because one or more salespeople missed theirs." While their perception of the obvious math was correct, what they failed to realize is that their region missed their numbers because they didn't effectively understand and manage each of their salespeople's inputs to achieve each of the salesperson's goals. Not all salespeople are the same. The inputs might be the same to produce a sale, but not all salespeople have the same strengths and weaknesses as regards those inputs. What I wanted to know from the sales managers was which of the underperforming salesperson's inputs needed to be improved and how the manager planned to coach each sales rep so that the sales rep's, the region's, and the manager's performance and scalability would improve going forward.

Managers in any department, not just sales, need to look in the mirror, especially when they decide to replace a nonperformer.

Why? Because if one of their direct reports failed, then so did the manager. The manager failed to hire the right person, failed to train and coach that person, and/or failed to identify that person's issues in time to create and coach them through a performance-improvement plan. At Cyberonics, every manager's turnover was tracked, reported, and reviewed quarterly so that senior management could help managers with high turnover lower that turnover by being better managers and coaches. The lower the turnover, the more scalable you and your company are.

The fifth building block of scalability is communication: Providing feedback and input and seeking feedback and input from those above, beside, and below you, including your significant other, your family, those working for you personally, your peers, your boss, and those higher than you in the organization at work. In essence, anyone and everyone who has an impact on your scalability and your personal and professional growth objectives. In general, regular communication with those working for you, including appropriate input, feedback, and coaching on their performance and what they can do to improve their performance is an essential part of effective management. As is you seeking the input, feedback, and coaching from all those at and outside of work who can positively or negatively affect your scalability and your achievement of your personal and professional growth plans.

If you're reading this book, you no doubt have aspirations and perhaps plans for personal and professional growth. If that's the case, then your personal scalability is very important to you. Your scalability will be one of the major determinants of how bright your future is and how much personal, professional, and financial abundance you will create and share.

CHAPTER 16
THE SELF-CARE TEST

Are you following the airlines' advice to put your oxygen mask on first?

WHY DO THE airlines tell us to put our own oxygen mask on first? Isn't it because we can't help others in the event of an emergency if we've suffocated? If you think about it, doesn't that advice apply to life in general? In order to have a positive effect on the world around us and improve the lives of others, we need to put on our oxygen mask first to prevent suffocation on every level: personal, emotional, intellectual, spiritual, professional, and financial. And not only to prevent suffocation, but also to become the best version of ourselves to maximize the positive energies, pleasure, bliss, and abundance we create and share.

How are you doing at taking care of the person in your life who will have the single biggest impact on you and those around you? Namely you. Taking care of you is an essential part of mastering you from the inside out, realizing your full potential, and creating and sharing abundance of all kinds. Here are a few questions to help you evaluate your self-care:

1. Do you love yourself unconditionally? Meaning at all times.

2. Do you forgive yourself for making mistakes?

3. Are you grateful to yourself and others for the positive things in your life, small and large?

4. How often do unreasonable expectations prevent you from being happy?

5. Do you give gifts, including your time, attention, cards, flowers, dinners out, and other intangible and tangible things unconditionally? Or do you expect something in return?

6. Do you receive gifts unconditionally with gratitude, meaning that you don't expect similar future gifts?

7. Are you happy with the way you look? The way you feel? Your mental, physical, emotional, and spiritual health?

8. Are you happy with your sex life?

9. Are you living with integrity or are you carrying around a guilty conscience?

10. When you're feeling stressed out, when you need a break, or in "case of an emergency," what do you do to put your oxygen mask on first? Keep doing what you're doing? Go for a run? Overeat "comfort" food? Drink? Get drunk? Go to the gym? Meditate? Take a vacation? Practice yoga? Go for a walk?

11. How is your "oxygen mask" different now than what it was five years ago? Have you stopped doing things that provided you invaluable oxygen that you wish you were still doing? Have you added new "oxygen mask" activities?

12. Think about a time when you put your oxygen
    mask on first and then helped others. And a time
    when you tried to help others without putting
    your oxygen mask on first. And a time when
    you put your oxygen mask on first and didn't
    help others. Were the outcomes different? Did
    you feel differently? In which situation were
    you happier? In which situation did you feel
    some resentment? In which situation did those
    around you seem to benefit most?

13. Think of a relationship you've had with
    your job, a loved one, or a friend in which
    you maintained minimal to no boundaries,
    subordinated your needs and wants to
    those of your partner, and accommodated,
    indulged, and accepted your partner's
    behavior regardless of how inappropriate,
    disrespectful, or abusive that behavior
    was. A relationship in which you never put
    your oxygen mask on first. How did that
    relationship work for you? How would the
    relationship have been different if you put
    your oxygen mask on first?

When I was young, I recall Grandma Bowie saying to me,
"You'll never love someone else until you love yourself." I have
no recollection of the context in which she said it or why. But
I've never forgotten what she said. And when I'm having a hard
time loving someone unconditionally, believing that they love
me unconditionally, accepting someone's apology and forgiving
them, or letting go of someone else's mistakes, I recall what she
said as if she were saying it to me right then and there. And that

recollection creates a funny feeling in my stomach—which is, of course, transmitted to my brain via the vagus nerve!

It seems as though many of us are taught to only hold those around us, including our kids, spouses, and coworkers to the same standards to which we hold ourselves. I know that's what I was taught. Lead by example, and expect from others only what you expect/demand of yourself. But what if the standards to which you hold yourself are unhealthy? Namely that you love yourself only with conditions, you never really forgive yourself for making a mistake or doing something that hurt you or those around you, or you never let go of anything you did that you consider to be wrong? If you treat others the same way you're treating yourself, you're probably not a very pleasant person to be around and you're likely only receiving from others what you're giving to them—conditional love and a lack of forgiveness.

The flight attendant in my life who finally convinced me to put my oxygen mask on first was my former wife of twenty-one years and the mother of my children. She did so after watching the Cyberonics' board, SunTrust, Wall Street, the SEC, the *New York Times*, the FDA not-approvable crowd, and others destroy my career, reputation, identity, self-esteem, and net worth, and me exist as a tortured zombie in the land of the living dead for four years until I finally received my closure letter from the SEC. She saved my life by giving me a hall-pass trip to Las Vegas to get my "mojo" back and by introducing me to tantra as a technique to let go of all the negative energy blocks I was carrying around.

During my four-day trip to Las Vegas, I observed a lot of people from a variety of cultures enjoying themselves and having fun. I also observed myself and began the process of figuring out who I really am and what really makes me happy. I began to understand what it meant to put my oxygen mask on first, and what, for me, constituted "oxygen."

Having always been an athlete who took care of his body and was nourished by being good at sports, when I returned to Texas, where I was living at the time, I put my oxygen mask on first by becoming an athlete again. I had laser liposuction to get rid of the tire around my middle, I did P90X workouts as if my life depended on it (which, figuratively, it did), and I started eating right. I then added testosterone therapy to improve my energy and mood and in one year was a totally new man. I was thirty-five pounds lighter and my waist was four inches smaller. And I was in the best shape of my life, physically, mentally, and emotionally. Instead of being bitter about what I lost, I learned to be grateful for who and what I was and all the blessings in my life, small and large. I felt good about and was grateful to and for *me* and as a result, I was a better husband, father, brother, and friend. I was also grateful to and for all those around me, and ready to continue my awakening and re-empowerment journey through the tantra oxygen mask.

My study of tantra yoga reinforced the importance of gratitude as a way of practicing unconditional self-love. Tantra also taught me the importance of giving unconditionally and renouncing attachment to the expected outcomes of my giving. Expectations are the precursors to resentment and disappointment. If you're giving a gift conditionally, you're doing so expecting something in return. You're trading whatever it is you're giving someone for something in return. Some form of "payment." One of my issues from whence I came was the disease to please and the disappointment and, at times, resentment I felt when I deemed inadequate the thanks and gratitude I received in return. The sequence that my inability to give gifts unconditionally would often create was (1) I would buy or create a special gift with a lot of forethought and effort, (2) I'd then give the gift with great joy, (3) when the recipient's joy and gratitude invariably didn't meet my expectations, I would be obviously upset, (4) the joy and happiness that both of us felt would disappear, and (5) both of us would hesitate when it came time to give and receive future gifts. When it came to giving, if I had "put my oxygen mask on first" and loved myself and my giving unconditionally without the attachment to outcomes, then my gifts could have brought everyone great joy. Instead, I didn't first take care of myself and gave to others expecting them to take care of me. Can you think of gifts that you've given unconditionally and those that you've given expecting something in return? Which made you happier?

Tantra also taught me that whenever someone receives your gifts unconditionally, without feeling as if they have to give you something in return, they are giving you the incredible gift of surrender. They are living in the moment and receiving your gifts without any expectation regarding future gifts. They are simply receiving all that you're sharing, expressing their gratitude by surrendering and sharing whatever pleasure and bliss they're feeling with you unconditionally. Giver becomes receiver and receiver becomes giver naturally through their unconditional giving, receiving, and surrender. Receiving a gift unconditionally means being grateful, expressing that gratitude, and not expecting similar future gifts.

When I learned how to put my oxygen mask on first by giving unconditionally, the pleasure and bliss I experienced as a gift from the receiver matched the pleasure and bliss I experienced by conceiving of, creating, and giving the gift. Especially in love-making. When I learned how to unconditionally honor, nurture, and worship my significant other even without traditional "sex," her pleasure and my pleasure went off the charts! Her pleasure became my pleasure, unlike anything I'd been previously taught or experienced.

Once you learn how to love yourself and give unconditionally, forgive yourself, abandon expectations and practice gratitude, you become a better parent, spouse, and manager/coworker. Needless to say, as outlined in this book, I've made my share of big mistakes and betrayed myself many times. Before I learned how to love myself unconditionally, forgive myself, have compassion for myself, and let go of things from my past that didn't serve me, my kids, my spouses, and the people who worked for me often thought they were never good enough and always were doing things "wrong." Why? Because that was the way I felt and thought about myself. I never gave myself a break, never gave myself the benefit of the doubt, never forgave myself. Of course I projected all those feelings onto others. If I only knew then what I know now!

The next time you feel yourself being critical of someone else, ask yourself if you are simply projecting your self-criticism onto that other person. If you're upset with your spouse/significant other and are saying to yourself, "I can't take this anymore," ask yourself if your inability to forgive and forget and/or love uncon- ditionally is because you can't forgive yourself, can't let go of your past mistakes, and/or don't love yourself unconditionally. You just might discover that your problem with your spouse or kids is really your problem with yourself and you haven't put your oxygen mask on first. The next time at work, when you look at someone and resent how good they look or how happy they are and rationalize those things as them not being as dedicated as you, think about whether your resentment is really directed toward yourself and your failure to put your oxygen mask on first.

Have you ever heard the term "codependency" or "codepen- dent relationship?" Have you ever been in a codependent relation- ship? Unfortunately, I didn't know those terms and therefore didn't think I had ever been in a codependent relationship. I now know that the from whence I came was codependency, which started when my mother's addictions told me that my needs didn't matter. Being true to thine own self and putting your oxygen mask on first is especially important if you're in a codependent relationship.

A codependent relationship is a one-sided relationship where one person relies on the other to satisfy all their wants and needs. Once thought to be a unique characteristic of spouses of alcoholics, codependents often enable their significant others to maintain addictive, irresponsible, and inappropriate behaviors. Codependents often subordinate all their needs and wants to those of their partner, children, etc., and make a disproportionate share of the compromises to maintain the relationship, and, as a result, often feel trapped.

Many codependents, because they have chosen to be codependent or refuse to get help for their codependency, feel as though their needs don't matter, feel compelled to please everyone but themselves, feel like they have to take care of or "fix" everyone around them, and maintain poor boundaries as regards money, their bodies, belongings, thoughts, and feelings. Codependents desperately need to be in personal and professional relationships in which they can be the "fixer" of others' problems to feel validated. Even if those relationships are abusive. Because codependents fear being abandoned or rejected, they go to great lengths to be liked and constantly seek the approval of others. Often in denial about their codependency, codependents blame others and circumstances for their feelings. They also can be resentful and angry toward those they can't fix or who don't want or heed their advice.

By always putting others first, you're repeatedly telling yourself and others that you and your needs don't matter. And, in some cases, that you have no personal or professional boundaries. Is that really the message you want to send? Codependency is the antithesis of putting your oxygen mask on first.

Putting your oxygen mask on first means taking the time to do those things that make you feel good about *you*. Take vacations. Go to the gym. Practice yoga. Meditate. Go skiing. Go for a run or bike ride. Watch a movie. Read a book. Go to a comedy club. Build some furniture. Maintain healthy personal and professional boundaries that do not accommodate or enable unacceptable behaviors. Whatever takes care of *you* and helps you become the best version of *you*. Sometimes being "selfish" with your time enables you to be selfless and give the most to others. Especially if you know from whence you came and are living with integrity. Putting your oxygen mask on first—with integrity—means that your intention is to take care of yourself so that you can not only become the best version of *you*, but also have a more positive effect on those around you in a nonzero-sum game in which everybody wins. If you put your own oxygen mask on first without any regard for what effect that will have on those around you, aren't you potentially doing so in a zero-sum game in which you win and those around you lose? And doing so without integrity in a narcissistic way?

At Cyberonics, I was a codependent workaholic. I traveled more than half the time and when I was home, I regularly worked twelve-plus hour days. I was always on call with my pager then mobile phone constantly nearby, interrupting time with my family, including every family vacation. Looking back on it, I was clearly in—and I dragged my family into—a codependent relationship with Cyberonics that I mistakenly thought validated me. All of my needs and my family's needs were secondary to those of Cyberonics and there was *always* something that needed to be "fixed" by *me* and *only me*.

At Cyberonics, our vacation policy for senior managers and vice presidents was to take as much vacation time as they needed (at least four weeks a year) to take care of themselves and their families and be as productive at work as possible when they returned. We asked that vacations be scheduled during non-crisis times when someone else in their departments or groups could cover for them. If a crisis forced someone to reschedule a vacation, Cyberonics paid the costs associated with rescheduling. Unfortunately I didn't practice what I was preaching because although my family and I took many wonderful vacations, my codependent relationship partner, Cyberonics, came along on every vacation via mobile phone, conference calls, emails, faxes, etc., etc. I was almost never fully present with my wife and family on vacation, robbing us of the joy, pleasure, and bliss we deserved had I known then what I know now. Not only do I understand what a codependent relationship is and how codependency can adversely impact my life, but I also know that if you're in a codependent relationship, that relationship can and will destory other relationships.

Are family vacations for you a way to put your oxygen mask on first? For me they weren't because I chose to make family vacations part of my suffocating codependent relationship with Cyberonics. My poor choice forced me to find an oxygen mask that didn't involve Cyberonics or my family.

Enter the three-day Derek Daly Academy car racing school in Las Vegas. By the second day I realized that I had found the oxygen mask that I desperately needed. I wasn't thinking about or communicating with Cyberonics. I wasn't thinking about my family except when we talked in the evenings. All I was thinking about was the car I was driving, the track, the data from the car's data acquisition system, and the inputs I needed to change to improve my lap times and go faster. Being fully present in the present not only created bliss for me, but also enabled me to quickly become one of the fastest students to ever attend the school. Desperate for lifesaving oxygen, I was now totally hooked.

Racing for me became a classic zero-sum-game oxygen mask. From 2000 to 2006, I spent more and more time at various race tracks and spent more and more money on more and more powerful cars, spares, haulers, including a fifty-three-foot brand-new Peterbilt, team gear, etc. First as an amateur racer then as a "professional," racing a Daytona prototype in the Rolex Series and stock cars in ARCA. Unlike all the other pro teams, we had no sponsors. Race weekends were costing me around $100,000 per weekend at the end of my "career." I am living proof of the old adage, "How do you make a small fortune in racing? Start with a big one." Unfortunately I didn't start with a "big one," so the small one in terms of time and money my family and I were left with was really small. A classic zero-sum-game oxygen mask in which the costs were primarily my family's and the benefits were primarily mine. Obviously I didn't understand then that with the privilege of putting my oxygen mask on first came the responsibility of helping others, especially those most important to me, with their oxygen masks.

Have you ever put your oxygen mask on first only to realize that it's a zero-sum-game mask? Zero-sum-game oxygen masks that reward you at the expense of others can be very expensive. My racing oxygen mask in many ways resembles Beck Weathers' mountain climbing oxygen mask that cost him his nose, one of his arms from the elbow down, and his other hand that he describes now as a "mitt." And nearly cost him his family and his life. Recall that Beck was the Dallas oncologist who was left for dead three times during the 1996 Mount Everest disaster. I first met Beck in 1997 when he was the keynote speaker at our epilepsy launch meeting following FDA approval, attended by some three hundred neurologists. You could have heard a pin drop while Beck told his story. The one person in the audience, who was sitting briefly next to me before she left, who wasn't thrilled, was Beck's wife. Looking back, she was obviously upset by Beck's mountain-climbing oxygen mask that provided him with all the rewards and his family with all the risks.

In a November 2017 video interview by the *Dallas Morning News* regarding *Everest*, the movie about the 1996 disaster, Beck provided all of us with some of his "if he only knew then what he knows now" wisdom derived from being left for dead three times at 28,000 feet on the side of Everest and being given a second chance. Most importantly by his wife, Peach, and his family. In that interview, Beck said he'd always been fairly obsessed with work, training for mountains, and his quest for the Seven Summits, but thanks to Everest, he now knows that "those kinds of behaviors make you successful" but alienate you from the most important people in your life, your family. He said that in the past, he'd been focused on the future, pursuing one goal after the other such that the future never arrived. Now he lives in the present and is a lot more peaceful, living comfortably in his own skin, not defining himself based on achievements alone. According to Beck, the oxygen mask he wore on Everest provided him with a serious wake-up call and saved his life.

I first came across Beck's video interview in late 2018 as I was writing this chapter. It hit me like a ton of bricks. I must have watched it 20 times and cried every time I watched it. Not because Beck's story didn't end well, but because I was too blind too see and too deaf to hear the real message and prophecy in Beck's 1997 talk and his wife's reaction. Beck's personal and professional life ascents were brought back to earth in a very dramatic way by Mount Everest, with much suffering for his wife, his children and Beck himself. When he gave his talk, my personal and professional life ascents at Cyberonics were just beginning. At the time, I was captivated by the glory of Beck's courageous quest and his story of survival. Too bad I didn't pay more attention to his wife's reaction and understand that Beck's story was a classic Greek tragedy in which a protagonist, usually an important person with outstanding personal qualities, falls to disaster through a combination of personal failings, like hubris, and insurmountable forces. Because my Everest—namely seeking approval to use VNS to treat depression—was coming. With disastrous consequences for millions of people whose lives were touched by treatment resistant illnesses, my family, and me. As if to unknowingly tempt fate, Cyberonics even used a photo showing the various camps and the climbing route up Everest to communicate where we were on our quest for depression approval!

Applying the airlines' oxygen mask instructions to life in general is just another way of saying that you will treat others the way you treat yourself. If you love yourself unconditionally, you will love others unconditionally. If you give to and receive from yourself unconditionally, you will do the same for others. If you forgive yourself and let go of events from the past that don't serve you, you will do the same for others. And you and those around you will be considerably happier and healthier.

So which oxygen mask do you think is better? One that is put on one of your loved ones by the YOU whose mask is already on or the YOU whose mask isn't on? One that is put on by the YOU who loves and respects yourself or the YOU who doesn't? The YOU who maintains healthy boundaries or the YOU who doesn't? The YOU who is obsessed by work and hobbies like car racing and mountain climbing? The YOU who feels liberated or the YOU that is suffocating and feels trapped? The YOU who knows that your needs matter or the YOU who thinks they don't? The YOU who is happy or the YOU who is resentful? The YOU who puts their mask on out of love or the YOU who feels obligated to do so?

Put your oxygen mask on first, then help others. Perhaps you'll inspire others to do the same.

CHAPTER 17

MENTORS, CONFIDANTES, AND OPM

My financial training and experience taught me that OPM means "other people's money." In this chapter it means "other people's mistakes."

WHAT DO YODA, the nine-hundred-year-old Jedi master of the *Star Wars* films, and Nick Foles, the former journeyman and second-string Eagles quarterback who won the 2017 Super Bowl MVP after the Eagles upset the New England Patriots, have in common? They both know the importance of embracing and learning from mistakes and failures, especially other people's mistakes and failures.

During his post-game interview, Foles, who nine months earlier was ready to quit football, was asked what he would like to share from his remarkable journey. I watched the interview live and will never forget his response:

"I think the big thing is don't be afraid to fail . . . In our society today—you know, Instagram, Twitter, it's a highlight reel. It's all the good things. And then when you look at it . . . when you have a rough day or you think, 'My life's not as good as that,' and you think you're failing. Failure is a part of life. That's a part of building character and growing . . . without failure, who would you be? I wouldn't be up here if I hadn't fallen thousands of times. Made mistakes . . . We all are human, we all have weaknesses . . . I know when I listen to people speak and they share their weaknesses [mistakes and failures], I'm [REALLY] listening . . . So I'm not perfect. I'm not Superman. I might be in the NFL, and we might have just won the Super Bowl but, hey . . . I still have daily struggles . . . If something's going on in your life and you're struggling? Embrace it, because you're growing."

The same goes for Yoda, who seems to know a thing or two about mastering you from the inside out. In *The Last Jedi*, Yoda says the following to Luke in a dream:

"Heeded my words, not, did you? Pass on what you have learned. Strength. Mastery. But weakness, folly, failure, also. Yes, failure most of all. The greatest teacher, failure is."

Success teaches us a lot, but as Super Bowl MVP Nick Foles and Jedi grand master Yoda said, mistakes and failures teach us more. A lot more. But, as I discuss throughout this book, mistakes and failures can be very, very costly—personally, professionally, emotionally, spiritually, and financially. There are two ways to learn from mistakes and failures. Make them and pay the full price of tuition. Like I did. Or learn from others' mistakes and failures and pay considerably less. Especially others, like a mentor or confidante who is not only willing to share his or her successes, but also— most importantly—unafraid to share mistakes and failures.

Let's take a look at your experience using mentors and confidantes and how much you've benefited from their willingness to share their mistakes and failures. Write down your answers to the following questions:

1. Who is your current work/career mentor or confidante? Does this mentor have relevant experience that helps you now or might help you in the future? How has your current work mentor helped you? What has your mentor shared with you about his or her mistakes and failures? Do you completely trust your work mentor? Are you willing to share everything with them? What won't you share? Could anything you share with them have a negative impact on your career or status at work? What has your mentor told you that you didn't want to hear? Does you mentor disagree with you when their experience is different than yours? What could your mentor do better? What traits would make for a better work mentor, such as working for a different company? Does your mentor seem interested in unconditionally providing you with the benefit of their experience? Or do they seem to be giving you advice that they expect you to take?

2. If you don't have a career/work mentor, why not?

3. Who was your mentor before the current one? How was that mentor different than your current one? How did your previous mentor help you? From which of your previous mentor's mistakes and failures did you benefit the most? Did you completely trust your

previous work mentor? Were you willing to share everything with this person? What wouldn't you share and why? How does your previous work/career mentor compare to your current one?

4. Who is your mentor/confidante outside work? Does this personal confidante have relevant knowledge and experiences that you believe will be beneficial to you? How has your personal confidante helped you? From which of your confidante's mistakes and failures have you learned the most? Do you completely trust your personal confidante? Are you totally confident that all your conversations will remain strictly confidential and won't go beyond the two of you? Are you willing to share everything with them? What won't you share? Does this mentor always agree with you and tell you what you want to hear? What has your mentor told you that you didn't want to hear? When have they disagreed with you? Could anything you share with them have a negative impact on your personal life? What could this mentor do better? What traits would make for a better personal confidante? Are they part of your family or in your circle of friends. Does your personal confidante seem to be interested in unconditionally providing you with the benefit of their experience? Or do they seem to be giving you advice that they expect you to take?

5. What specific mistakes and failures from your past do you think a trusted, experienced, been

there, done that mentor/confidante could have helped you avoid?

6. What issues are you currently, or do you anticipate facing, in your career, at work, and in your personal life that a trusted, experienced, been there, done that confidante/mentor's experience could help you navigate?

7. Given your answers to the previous questions, what traits and characteristics does your ideal mentor/confidante have?

The single most important lesson that all my successes, accomplishments, mistakes, and failures have taught me is that the only way to have known then what I know now was to have confidantes/mentors who had already experienced what I was about to experience, already made mistakes similar to the ones I was about to make, and already failed in similar ways as I was about to fail. So I could learn from them. And maximize success while minimizing mistakes and failures.

Throughout most of my life, I never really used mentors or confidantes. There are many reasons why. First was my programmed reliance on me, myself, and I. Second was probably ego. I didn't admit to myself that I could use help in the form of someone else's knowledge and experience. Another reason is that I didn't understand the extent to which I needed help. That is until eighteen months ago, when I discovered that I needed a been there, done that, seen many successes, mistakes, and failures consultant, confidante, and mentor to help me help you to master you from the inside out.

One of the many things I know now thanks in large part to writing this book is what for me constitutes the "right" versus "wrong" mentor or confidante. My list of traits for the "ideal" mentor or confidante is as follows:

1. They have highly relevant, broad, and deep personal and professional experience. Meaning they've been there, done that when it comes to where I've been, where I am, and where I'm going in life.

2. They are willing to share their successes, but more importantly, mistakes and failures with me.

3. The more successful you are personally and professionally, the more people you will intimidate. You will be surrounded by "yes" men and women. As a result, my ideal mentor/ confidante is a person who is willing to tell me what I don't want to hear and provide me with a totally different perspective when necessary.

4. Their only relationship with me is as a mentor or confidante. We don't work together. We don't socialize together. We don't have common friends, etc.

5. Our relationship is completely confidential. They don't disclose our relationship or anything we've talked about to anyone without my permission.

6. They don't judge me.

7. I trust them and as a result feel comfortable telling them everything and anything.

8. Their goal is simply to share with me all their relevant experience to facilitate me

making the best, most informed decisions possible. They mentor me by asking me a lot of questions and providing me with all their relevant experience. To use the old fishing adage, they watch me fish, they ask me a lot of questions about my fishing plans, goals, and techniques, and they provide me with all of their relevant fishing successes, mistakes, and failures. Then they let me do the fishing. They don't fish for me. They don't tell me how to fish and they don't get offended if I don't fish "their way."

Think about how many people's lives are impacted by the thousands of decisions each of us makes personally and professionally throughout our lifetimes. The number of lives each of us touches is staggering. The right confidantes/mentors help us make better decisions. The better our decisions, the more we improve the staggering number of lives touched by those decisions. And the more abundance of all kinds—emotional, personal, intellectual, professional, and financial—we create and share.

The right confidantes/mentors who knew then much of what I know now would have likely helped me, among other things:

1. Create, build, and maintain stronger and healthier mutually beneficial personal and professional relationships.

2. Preserve my twenty-one-year marriage to the mother of my children and keep intact the family we created.

3. Continue to grow my personal and professional reputation and career before, during, and after Cyberonics.

4. Improve the lives of millions of people touched by treatment-resistant epilepsy, depression, and other disorders, the lives of people who invested in or worked for or were suppliers to or customers of Cyberonics and other companies I started, and worked for, was on the board of, and/or invested in post-Cyberonics.

5. Create and share significantly more joy, happiness, pleasure, bliss, and abundance of all kinds with the world around me.

6. Realize my share of the value I created and would be continuing to create for others.

How would the right mentor or confidante have helped me do those things? And how can the right confidantes and mentors help you? This book, in many ways a written mentor and confidante, provides you with some ideas. I would be happy to tell and show you even more at skipcummins.com.

Thank you for sharing your time with me. I hope you found our time together worthwhile. Good luck on your quest to master you from the inside out. Extraordinary abundance of all kinds awaits you.

ACKNOWLEDGEMENTS

THIS BOOK STARTS with the tragic suicide of my mother. Never in my wildest imagination did I think it would end with another devastating family tragedy. But it did. The sudden, unexpected and shocking death of my daughter, Linda, on September 15, 2019, the day after her thirty-second birthday. I thought I knew the depths of grief when my mother died. I didn't. I know now.

Without Linda, I would have never written this book. She encouraged and inspired me to never give up regardless of how many paragraphs or chapters I had to rewrite. She read every word of every draft and provided me with invaluable feedback. She reminded me constantly that every word I was writing and the experiential knowledge I was sharing was important. She gave me space when I needed space. She offered kind words of encouragement when I needed them. And she pushed, really hard when I needed to be pushed. At those times she reminded me of more than a few football coaches I had in my life. She knew me well. And loved me. As I did her.

I first met Linda in 1995 when she was 8 years old, shortly before her mother Baiba accepted my proposal of marriage and Linda simultaneously accepted my proposal to join Baiba and Linda's family. In 1996 our new family became official when Baiba and I were married and shortly thereafter Linda legally adopted me as her dad. It was my first time as a dad and I will be eternally grateful to Baiba and Linda for giving me that privilege and honor.

I'll never forget the first time Linda called me "dad," just before she adopted me. I was filled with a joy and love I had never known.

Linda amazed me. Always incredibly happy and loving. A friend to every creature on god's green earth, human and otherwise. Every day for her was a new adventure. Every new thing she learned was a blessing. Every person she met was a friend. She loved and gave of herself more freely than I thought possible.

She quickly became her daddy's little girl. And my very special friend. We did everything together. Initially from our first home as a family in Edwards CO some 15 miles west of Vail.

I taught Linda and Baiba to ski while riding my snowboard and like with everything else, she learned very quickly. I remember one day Linda and I went skiing at Beaver Creek with over two feet of fresh powder. It continued to snow while we skied all day until the lifts closed. The snow was up to Linda's chest and we had to ski the steepest runs just to move. She stayed four feet behind me turn after turn as if she was tethered to me with a rope. All the while glowing with joy and smiling her famous Linda smile. The few people riding the chair above us were amazed at Linda and shouted words of encouragement to her such as" go girl go." What a day.

We continued to ski together even after she became a better skier than me, including on three helicopter skiing trips in Canada. I felt an indescribable sense of peace, happiness and accomplishment watching her ski and feeling the total freedom and bliss she was experiencing doing something I taught her to do then watching her befriend everyone in the lodge, staff and guests included. Not needing me to do either one.

Another of my fondest memories of Linda is with her first "real" bike which we bought her in the spring of 1996. Of course it was purple, her favorite color. We had a relatively steep quarter mile driveway and there was a 2.5 mile hilly loop around the gated development where we lived. Linda helped me get into very good shape because she never wanted to get off her bike and wanted me to run or bike around the loop with her constantly.

One thing you must know about Linda is that coming from the "old country" and being raised by her mother, she never thought she was entitled to anything and never asked for anything. She was incredibly grateful for everything she was given most importantly time, attention and love. Material things weren't important to her.

Back to the bike story. One day I noticed her looking at the bike computer on my bike. I asked her if she knew what it was. She said no and I explained it to her. That is was used to measure speed, distance and pedal rpms on long bike rides. Her eyes further widened with my every word. I then asked her if she would like a computer for her bike. She then shyly with this huge grin on her face said, "yes please!" I then made her a deal. Since bike computers were tools to measure various things on long bike rides, I told her that I would get her a bike computer as soon as she could ride from our house all around the loop and back to our house without stopping. Not an easy ride. She grinned and said DEAL and we shook hands. One week later after working incredibly hard without complaint, she had her bike computer. She was proud to have it and I was even more proud of her for earning it.

One last memory. Linda LOVED and I mean loved horses and dogs. Shortly after we came together as a family I brought a giant schnauzer puppy which we named Otto back from New York. When he came off the plane in Denver he was covered in vomit, pee and poop. Linda didn't care. She hugged and talked to him, whispering sweet nothings in his ear for 3 hours back to Edwards. She then became a world champion dog trainer. When Otto was doing something he wasn't supposed to do Linda would giggle that Linda giggle of hers and say, "No, Otto, no," then giggle some more. Which of course only encouraged Otto to keep doing what he was doing and Linda to giggle even more. And me to laugh and compliment her on her dog training skills. Linda and Otto were a perfect match. Boundless energy and joy, and love of life and everything around them.

So that brings me unfortunately back to the present.

To say that I remain in total shock and disbelief is beyond a gross understatement.

Although Linda will live on in our memories, her incredibly bright light which touched and improved thousands of human and animal lives all over the world was snuffed out way too early.

She died of cardiac arrest sometime before 9pm while the fellow veterinarian whom she loved and invited to live with her in her home was playing video games. She was a perfectly healthy woman, veterinarian, daughter, sister, niece, and friend who had just celebrated her 32nd birthday the day before. Needless to say there are many unanswered questions regarding the causes of her cardiac arrest, the answers to which we expect to have soon.

If there is one lesson we should all take away from this unspeakable tragedy so that Linda doesn't die in vain it's this:

As Aesop said, "A man is known by the company he keeps." Or more appropriately given recent events, "a person is known by and their future and life depends on the company they keep." Meaning associate with, trust, love and share your life ONLY with those who:

- elevate you higher into your light
- help you realize your full potential personally and professionally
- haven't lied to you or cheated on you
- inspire you
- encourage you to grow

- help you spread your wings and fly
- celebrate your accomplishments
- are committed to reciprocity in your relationship on every level, personally, professionally, spiritually and financially, and
- your family and best friends like, trust and respect.

Apply Linda's lesson not only to yourself but also to those that you love, your parents, children, best friends, by intervening in their relationships that don't meet these criteria. As Linda taught us it can be a matter of life and death.

Thank you Linda for everything that you generously shared with me, your family, your friends, your patients, your school and work colleagues and the universe in general. There will never be another human being and soul like you. You will live forever in our hearts and the pages of this book. Rest in peace and fly free my beautiful daughter.

LINDA CUMMINS WEST, DVM

SEPTEMBER 14, 1987 – SEPTEMBER 15, 2019

DR LINDA WEST, DVM of Arlington TX passed away unexpectedly on September 15, 2019, one day after her 32nd birthday.

Linda was born Linda Getlina on September 14, 1987 in Riga, Latvia when Latvia was part of the Soviet Union. In pursuit of the American dream, Linda and her mother Baiba emigrated to the United States in 1991 when Linda was three and a half years old. Neither of them spoke any English, Baiba didn't know how to drive a car and they arrived in their new home country with three suitcases, $60 and a place to stay in the home of a relative in Winston Salem NC.

In 1996, when Linda was eight, she and Baiba welcomed Robert "Skip" Cummins into their family when Baiba and Skip married in Beaver Creek CO. Linda started calling Skip "Dad" shortly after the marriage and he officially became Linda's father when he adopted her in the fall of that year.

Linda took full advantage of the extraordinary educational opportunities in America. She graduated from The Kincaid School in Houston, TX with high honors in 2006, Dartmouth College with a BA in Mathematics in 2010 and a Doctor of Veterinary Medicine (DVM) from the Texas A&M College of Veterinary Medicine and Biomedical Sciences in 2017.

Linda received many awards and honors including as a member of the Dartmouth Equestrian team, as a classical pianist, as a kart racer, and as a student. Prior to earning her DVM in 2017, she studied or worked in Brussels, Belgium, St Petersburg, Russia, South Africa where she did veterinary work in various game preserves, Steamboat Colorado where she was a ski instructor, and in Houston TX where she was an analyst Reasoning Minds.

After graduation from A&M, Linda joined the Creature Comfort Animal Clinic in Arlington TX as a veterinarian. She was totally dedicated to the practice of veterinary medicine, loved working at Creature Comfort and loved providing care and compassion to pets of all kinds and their owners. Linda had many passions. The piano, puzzles, skiing, scuba diving, travel, horseback riding, cooking, entertaining, and her five dogs.

She is survived by her mother Baiba and her brother, Max in TX, her father Skip in Las Vegas, NV, two aunts in Cumming GA and two aunts and an uncle in Latvia.

ABOUT THE AUTHOR

SKIP HAS LIVED a life full of opportunities of a lifetime at full throttle, following his maybe wrong but never in doubt philosophy. A life full of extraordinary successes and accomplishments, devastating tragedies, and spectacular mistakes and failures. All of which he owns, has embraced, is grateful for and from which he has learned many valuable lessons. Both personally and professionally.

Skip was raised by his figurative "grandmother" on $12.50 per month of child support in a small town in Western Pennsylvania after his parents' third and final divorce. He was the first person from his small town to graduate from an Ivy League college, where he excelled at both football and track as a linebacker and javelin thrower.

Skip had an accomplished career, building and managing a $750 million venture capital company. He then became the CEO of an essentially bankrupt company, commercializing new medical science and a revolutionary new device for the treatment of drug resistant epilepsy and severe depression which improved the lives of hundreds of thousands of people and created over $1 billion in shareholder value.

Skip holds the distinction of receiving the Lifetime Achievement Award from the National Epilepsy Foundation while simultaneously being labeled as "the most combative CEO in America" by a Wall Street TV personality.

CPSIA information can be obtained
at www.ICGtesting.com
Printed in the USA
FSHW010314090420
68977FS